Receiving the Holy Spirit Today

Receiving the Holy Spirit Today

Victor Paul Wierwille

A study of
how to receive the holy spirit, *pneuma hagion*,
"power from on high, " and the
various manifestations and operations of that spirit

American Christian Press
New Knoxville, Ohio 45871

Other books by Victor Paul Wierwille

Are the Dead Alive Now?
Power for Abundant Living
The Bible Tells Me So
    Volume I, Studies in Abundant Living
The New, Dynamic Church
    Volume II, Studies in Abundant Living
The Word's Way
    Volume III, Studies in Abundant Living

Standard Book Number ISBN 0-910068-00-3
Library of Congress Catalog Card Number 73-176282
American Christian Press
New Knoxville, Ohio 45871
Sixth Edition
Published 1972
Printed in the United States of America

Dedicated to those

who

    have longed . . . yet doubted

     have hoped . . . yet feared

      have hungered . . . yet remain unsatisfied

who

    desire to receive today

     the gift from the Holy Spirit

      in all its fullness.

Receiving The Holy Spirit Today

by Victor Paul Wierwille

In the late 1960's and early 70's a sudden surge of curiosity and interest has swept the country concerning the gift from the Holy Spirit. Speaking in tongues, one of the nine manifestations of the gift of holy spirit, has caused no small fury in the organized church while getting increasing coverage by the mass media.

While certain groups and individuals are evidencing speaking in tongues and perhaps some other manifestations, little concrete knowledge about the gift of holy spirit is available to those who are seeking to receive, or to those who are wondering about the exact significance of what they are manifesting.

Receiving the Holy Spirit Today is dedicated to "those who have longed — yet doubted, have hoped — yet feared, have hungered — yet remain unsatisfied." The sincere and searching have found the answer to their needs and prayers in this book.

Receiving the Holy Spirit Today is a how-to-do-it book. It is also an in-depth Biblical study of the Holy Spirit field.

- What is the gift of holy spirit?
- Who is qualified to receive the holy spirit?
- How does one receive the holy spirit?
- What is speaking in tongues — and what is its purpose?
- Common fears about receiving the gift of holy spirit.
- A study of the five cases in Acts where groups and individuals received and manifested the holy spirit.
- A study of I Corinthians 12, 13, and 14.

Receiving the Holy Spirit Today is comprehensive, yet written with simplicity; carefully researched, yet explained in a down-to-earth fashion. This book is a *must* for every Christian who wants to tap into the Holy Spirit — and yet not do it in darkness, fear and frustration caused by lack of teaching from God's Word.

The Scripture used throughout this book is quoted from the King James Version unless otherwise noted. All explanatory insertions by the author within a Scripture verse are enclosed in brackets. All Greek words are italicized and printed with English letters.

Contents

SECTION THREE

APPENDIXES

Preface

When I was serving my first congregation, a Korean missionary asked me, "Why don't you search for the greatest of all things in life which would teach Christian believers the *how* of a real victorious life?" This challenge was the beginning of a search which led me through many, many hours of examining different English translations, the various critical Greek texts and Aramaic "originals," looking for the source of the power which was manifested in the early Church.

Finally I realized that the experience referred to as "receiving the Holy Spirit" in the Scriptures *was* and *is* actually available to every born-again believer today. I believed to receive the gift of holy spirit and I, too, manifested.

Ever since receiving into manifestation the holy spirit, I have had the desire to put in written form the longings and fears that were mine regarding the receiving thereof. Sharing my quest with the believers who are today seeking to be endued with power from on high may be instrumental in leading them to the answer of their heart's desire.

I knew from the Bible that what God sent at Pentecost was still available. It had to be, for God does not change. I knew that the receiving of the power from on high on the day of Pentecost had meant increased ability for the apostles and disciples years ago, and that I needed and wanted the same blessing. I knew that if the Church ever needed the holy spirit in manifestation it needed it now.

Throughout my academic training in a college, a university, four seminaries, from the commentaries I studied and from my years of questing and research among the various religious groups claiming adherence to the holy spirit's availability, there appeared many things contradictory to the accuracy of the recorded Word of God. I knew their teachings were sincere, but sincerity is no guarantee for truth.

The Word of God is Truth. I prayed that I might put aside all I had heard and thought out myself, and I started anew with the Bible as my handbook as well as my textbook. I did not want to omit, deny or change any passage for, the Word of God being the

Will of God, the Scripture must fit like a hand in a glove.

If you are a Christian believer, I sincerely encourage you to study this book. Do not allow your past teachings or feelings to discourage you from going on to receive God's best. If you need power and ability to face up to the snares of this life, you may find your answer while reading this book. It is my prayer that you may be edified, exhorted and comforted.

For those searching the Scriptures, desiring to know the reasons why, how, what or where, I suggest you do a careful study of the Introduction as well as the Appendix in this volume. For those who simply desire to receive, read chapters 1 through 5 and enjoy His great presence and power.

II Timothy 2:15:
Study to shew thyself approved unto God, a workman that needeth not to be ashamed, rightly dividing the word of truth.

To his helpers and colleagues every writer owes a profound debt. This sixth edition has been read and studied carefully by men and women of Biblical and spiritual ability. To all of these I am most grateful.

Introduction

A word of explanation is needed for those who have not previously been introduced to the idea that a greater understanding of the meaning of the Holy Scriptures may be received through comparing our English versions with the Greek manuscripts from which the English versions were translated.

I believe that the Word of God is Truth, so we must search beyond the Authorized Version or any other version for The Word as it was originally divinely inspired. This each believer can do. Even if a believer has no reading knowledge of the Greek or Aramaic languages, he is still able to check the accuracy of The Word when he is given the Greek or Aramaic words in English letters as I have done in this book. I believe you will be thrilled at the deeper understanding of the Scriptures which can be yours through this type of comparison.

When it comes to a study of the Greek noun *pneuma,* translated "spirit," a difficulty presents it-

1

self. In Greek manuscripts the word *pneuma* is never capitalized. Some nouns do not affect the sense of a passage of Scripture whether they are capitalized or not, but this is not true of the word *pneuma*. "Spirit" with an upper case *S* and "spirit" with a lower case *s* are two different things. Thus, when the word *pneuma* is translated "Spirit" with a capital *S* it is an interpretation rather than a translation, and as such is of no higher authority than the person or translator giving it.

The editors of printed editions of the Greek New Testament differ among themselves as to the use of capital letters for the word *pneuma*. In other words, when should *pneuma* be translated "Spirit" with a capital *S*, and when should it be "spirit" with a small *s*? We can get little or no help from the Authorized King James Version nor the Revised Version nor the Greek manuscripts; nor can we get any help from the printed Greek texts nor the Aramaic Peshitta text.

In our Authorized King James Version the word *pneuma* is used 385 times. It is translated with a capital *S*, Spirit — 133 times; *s*, spirit — 153; spiritual — 1; ghost — 2; life — 1; wind — 1; spiritually — 1; and with the word *hagion*, holy, it is rendered Holy Spirit 4 times and Holy Ghost 89 times.

2

If, however, we note the different forms of the word *pneuma* employed in the New Testament and the variations of usage of this word in its context in the Scriptures, we will gain a thorough understanding of all the nuances of meanings of the word *pneuma*. It is only then that we receive a more accurate understanding of the meaning of *pneuma*.

Since God means what He says and says what He means and has a meaning for everything He says, surely one cannot translate each usage of the Greek words *pneuma hagion* as "the Holy Spirit" or "the Holy Ghost" inserting the article "the" at will when there is none in the early manuscripts nor in the critical Greek texts. Translators of every English edition not only have added the article "the," but they have also taken the liberty of adding a capital *H*, a capital *S* and a capital *G* at will.

The plan of this work is to give every reader the Greek word or words as translated into English. In this way the reader may see for himself the exact word or words used in the early manuscripts and texts in every verse of Scripture. For more detailed information regarding the inherent and inerrant accuracy of the Word of God on each of the 385 verses where the word *pneuma* is used in the New Testament, refer to Appendix III.

When we consider the Greek words *pneuma hagion*

without the article "the," as seen in more than fifty passages in the critical Greek texts of the New Testament, we discover that these words are *never once* used in the sense of "the Holy Spirit," who is God, the Giver. Thus, *pneuma hagion*, when referring to that which came on the day of Pentecost, ought always to be translated with a small *h* and a small *s*. *Pneuma hagion* as used in the New Testament regarding that which was received into manifestation on the day of Pentecost always refers to what the Giver, the Holy Spirit, God, gave. A verse in John 3 will illustrate this clearly.

John 3:6:
... that which is born of the Spirit [the *pneuma*, Spirit, God] is spirit [*pneuma*].

The *Giver* is God, the Spirit. His *gift* is spirit. Failure to recognize the difference between the *Giver* and His *gift* has caused no end of confusion in the Holy Spirit field of study as well as in the understanding of the new birth.

The gift from The Holy Spirit, *the Giver*, is *pneuma hagion*, holy spirit, power from on high, spiritual abilities, enablements. This power is spirit in contrast to the senses. Spirit is holy as opposed to the flesh, which is called by God unholy. God is Holy Spirit and *God can only give that which He is;* there-

4

fore, the *gift* from the *Giver* is of necessity *holy* and *spirit*.

The gift is holy spirit, *pneuma hagion,* which is an inherent spiritual ability, *dunamis,* power from on high. This gift is "Christ in you, the hope of glory" with all its fullness.

Pneuma hagion, as used in the New Testament beginning with the day of Pentecost, refers to that which is received at the time of salvation and to the internal reception of the nine evidences or manifestations, miscalled the "gifts."

The Greek word *dunamis,* translated "power," is not power put forth or manifested, but inherent power received, spiritual ability given to the believer. *Exousia,* the Greek word from which we get our English word "exercise," is our God-given authority and right as born-again sons of God to exercise *dunamis,* which is to put our inherent power into operation. This power, however, will be manifested only to the extent that our minds are renewed and we act upon what has been received. Think of *dunamis,* power, as the potential energy received when we receive the holy spirit, *pneuma hagion.* It is energy within but doing no work. Therefore it is of no practical use — like the horsepower in a car when the automobile is standing still. There is another word, *energēmata,* which is translated "workings" or "operations." *Energēmata* is like kinetic energy, which is *dunamis* in use or operation. The Scriptures give nine operations, *energēmata,* which are the workings of this potential energy, *dunamis,* as power. When a believer exercises, *exousia,* his full authority as a son of God, this potential energy, *dunamis,* is put to work and is then manifested in the outward world of the senses. Thus, the holy spirit, *pneuma hagion,* "power from on high," is put into operation by the will of man which in turn produces the manifestations of the spirit, being energized by the Holy Spirit, who is God.

John 14, was spoken before Pentecost and speaks of the spirit.

John 14:17:
... for he dwelleth with you, and shall be in you.

At the time of the events of John 14 this *pneuma hagion* which was promised had not yet been given. Just prior to His ascension, Jesus instructed the apostles not to depart from Jerusalem, but to tarry there until the gift of holy spirit had been poured out.

Acts 1:4,5:
... wait for the promise of the Father, which, *saith he,* ye have heard of me.

6

For John truly baptized with water; but ye shall be baptized with the Holy Ghost not many days hence.

Thus, we know that the receiving of *pneuma hagion* is the same as or equal to "the promise of the Father." Further instruction is given in Luke.

Luke 24:49:
... I send the promise of my Father upon you: but tarry ye in the city of Jerusalem, until ye be endued [clothed or arrayed] with power [*dunamis*, spiritual ability] from on high.

Therefore, *pneuma hagion*, "the promise of the Father," is "power from on high," the receiving of which is to be baptized with the holy spirit, *pneuma hagion*.

We are now clear on exactly *what* came on the day of Pentecost and on the absolute meaning of *pneuma hagion* as "power from on high," which is inherent spiritual power, *dunamis*. It was the *gift* from the *Giver* which came at Pentecost, *pneuma hagion*, and should always be understood as such and translated with a small *h* and a small *s*.

We must constantly remember that Pentecost was the first time in the history of civilization that it was

7

possible for anyone to be born again. Jesus Christ came to make the new birth available. It was not available until Christ had fulfilled His mission. If this were not true, Christ lived, died and arose in vain, for then all could have been born again without the sacrifice of Christ. It is certain that we cannot have something before it is available and the new birth was not available until Pentecost. Pentecost launched the Church of the Body and those who were born again by grace were the first members of the new fellowship. Yet, it was not fully revealed what they had received until some years later when the "mystery which was kept secret since the world began" was revealed to Paul. (Romans 16:25,26; Ephesians 3:5,9; 5:32; Colossians 1:25—27; I Corinthians 2:1—10).

In Acts we read about the power of the holy spirit.

> Acts 1:8:
> ... ye shall receive power, after that the Holy Ghost [the *hagion pneuma*, POWER FROM ON HIGH, the gift] is come upon you ....

The English word "receive" has also caused a great deal of confusion in the Holy Spirit field. A problem in semantics has arisen because of different meanings and usages of words. The word "receive" may be used in the sense of receiving something spiritually as well as receiving something into manifestation in the world of the senses.

There are two Greek words translated "receive" which must be accurately defined and understood. These Greek words are *dechomai* and *lambanō*. From checking each usage in the New Testament the following are the exact meanings: *dechomai* is a subjective reception indicating that by a person's own decision something spiritual has taken place; *lambanō* is an objective reception indicating that by a person's decision he manifests outwardly that which has been received inwardly. In other words, to receive spiritually is *dechomai*, and to receive into manifestation in the senses world is *lambanō*. Thus, one can receive something spiritually, *dechomai*, without receiving it into manifestation, *lambanō*, in the senses world.

In Acts 8:14 and 15 both Greek words for "receive" are used.

Acts 8:14,15:
Now when the apostles ... heard that Samaria had received [*dechomai* — spiritually] the word of God [in other words, they were spiritually saved, for they believed according to verses 12 and 13], they sent unto them Peter and John:

Who, when they were come down, prayed for them, that they might receive [*lambanō* — mani-

9

fest in the senses world] the Holy Ghost
[*pneuma hagion*].

Thus, one can readily see that a knowledge of the
exact word is necessary to understand the significance
of the word "receive." It is possible to receive something spiritually without ever receiving it into
manifestation; however, one must receive [*dechomai*]
spiritually before one can receive into evidence or
manifestation [*lambanō*] in the senses world. The
word "receive" in verses 17 and 19 of Acts 8 is
*lambanō.**

It is of utmost importance to be keenly aware that
the Spirit, the Giver, is God and that his gift is power
from on high.

Acts 2:4:
And they were all filled with the Holy Ghost
[*pneuma hagion*, the gift, power from on high],
and began to speak with other tongues, as the
Spirit [the *pneuma*, the Giver] gave them utterance.

The Holy Spirit, God, was not *with* what they were
filled, but *by* whom they were filled, which made it
possible for *them* to speak in tongues. *What* they

*See Appendix I, page 259, for every Scripture reference in the
New Testament where *lambanō* or *dechomai* is used.

spoke was as the Spirit, the *Giver,* God, gave it to them – not to their minds but to their *pneuma,* spirit, which was His gift. Once given by God and received by man, the gift becomes the responsibility of the recipient, thus it is the believer's spirit.

The holy spirit, *pneuma hagion,* which was both received spiritually and received into manifestation in the senses world on the day of Pentecost is referred to in the Word of God by several different terms: "the promise of the Father," "the power from on high," to be "baptized with the Holy Ghost," "the gift of God." This book sets forth for its readers the study and explanation of this gift.

SECTION ONE

This section is primarily designed to aid the seeker in receiving the gift from the Holy Spirit, which many have longed to do. I have endeavored to present the receiving of this wonderful power so that everyone who sincerely desires to receive may do so.

I trust that the simplicity of this study will be its best recommendation. Coming through all the tangled mass of religious teaching on the Holy Spirit, I have emerged with the conviction and assurance that all truth in its least common denominator is easily understood. Theological cloaking makes the simplicity of The Word difficult. This study is, however, not oversimplified, I assure you, because that would tend toward error. When we carry out the Biblical admonition to become like little children, we can receive into manifestation the fullness of the power from the Holy Spirit.

CHAPTER ONE

The Gift from the Holy Spirit

Have you received the holy spirit, the power from on high? Many Christians believe that *pneuma hagion,* holy spirit, is automatically received at the time of salvation. They believe that when a person confesses Jesus Christ as his personal Lord and Savior, he receives eternal life which is *pneuma hagion,* holy spirit. This is not the whole truth. Apparently there is something more after salvation for the Christian to receive into manifestation, *lambanō.*

When speaking to the apostles, Christ made a distinction between the spirit being *with* and being *in.* John 14:17, spoken before Pentecost, says of the *pneuma* "... for he dwelleth with you [active present tense] and shall be in you [future tense]." As the *pneuma,* the *new birth* spirit, and as *pneuma hagion,* the power from on high, it entered into the apostles at Pentecost.

Without the working of the Holy Spirit, no one can be saved. After conversion or salvation, however, the Word of God plainly teaches that there is an act of receiving into manifestation the holy spirit. The primary purpose of receiving the holy spirit into manifestation is to give us power for abundant living. As Acts 1:8 says, "But ye shall receive power, after that the Holy Ghost [the *hagion pneuma*] is come upon you."

The act of receiving into manifestation *pneuma hagion* after being saved is clearly set forth in Acts.

Acts 8:14–19:
Now when the apostles which were at Jerusalem heard that Samaria had received the word of God, they sent unto them Peter and John:

Who, when they were come down, prayed for them, that they might receive the Holy Ghost [*pneuma hagion*]:

(For as yet he was fallen upon none of them: only they were baptized in the name of the Lord Jesus.)

Then laid they *their* hands on them, and they received [*lambanō*] the Holy Ghost [*pneuma hagion*].

16

The Gift from the Holy Spirit

And when Simon saw that through laying on of the apostles' hands the Holy Ghost [the *pneuma the hagion*] was given, he offered them money,

Saying, Give me also this power, that on whomsoever I lay hands, he may receive [*lambanō*] the Holy Ghost [*pneuma hagion*].

The people of Samaria to whom Philip had preached the gospel were saved, and yet not one received into manifestation the power from on high, *pneuma hagion*. But when Peter and John laid hands on them, the Samaritans did receive into manifestation.

In the situation at Samaria we have clear and concise evidence that those who were saved needed to receive into evidence in the senses world the holy spirit, *pneuma hagion*. Something more was available than what they had received at the time of their salvation. This added spiritual blessing was their legal right according to the command given on the day of Pentecost.*

In speaking to the Ephesians, Paul was concerned

---

*Acts 2:38,39: "Then Peter said unto them, Repent, and be baptized every one of you in the name of Jesus Christ for the remission of sins, and ye shall receive the gift of the Holy Ghost. For the promise is unto you, and to your children, and to all that are afar off, *even* as many as the Lord our God shall call.

about one question only: "Have ye received [*lambanō*] the Holy Ghost [*pneuma hagion*] since [when] ye believed?"

Acts 19:1–6:
And it came to pass, that, while Apollos was at Corinth, Paul having passed through the upper coasts came to Ephesus: and finding certain disciples,

He said unto them, Have ye received the Holy Ghost [*pneuma hagion*] since ye believed? And they said unto him, We have not so much as heard whether there be any Holy Ghost [*pneuma hagion*].

And he said unto them, Unto what then were ye baptized? And they said, Unto John's baptism.

Then said Paul, John verily baptized with the baptism of repentance, saying unto the people, that they should believe on him which should come after him, that is, on Christ Jesus.

When they heard *this*, they were baptized in the name of the Lord Jesus.

And when Paul had laid *his* hands upon them, the Holy Ghost [the *pneuma hagion*] came on them; and they spake with tongues, and prophesied.

Paul expected believers to receive the holy spirit into manifestation. They were first instructed by Apollos in Jesus Christ and when they believed, they were saved. Later, Paul laid his hands on them and they received into manifestation *pneuma hagion,* holy spirit, the power from on high, and spoke in tongues and prophesied.

It is a commonly accepted truth among Biblical believers that the age of the Church started at Pentecost. Peter preached the first recorded sermon on the day of Pentecost and at the conclusion of the message the people responded by saying, "What shall we do?"

Acts 2:38:
Then Peter said unto them, Repent, and be baptized every one of you in the name of Jesus Christ for the remission of sins, and ye shall receive [*lambanō*] the gift of the Holy Ghost [*pneuma hagion*].

This procedure, given by Peter under the direction of the Holy Spirit, is the order for the age of the Church of the Body. The explanation is self-evident if we take The Word as written without removing it from its context.

According to Acts 1:4 and 5, Jesus commanded His apostles to receive the holy spirit, *pneuma hagion*. In Matthew 28:19 and 20, Jesus instructed His disciples to go and teach "all things whatsoever I have commanded you." He commanded them to tarry until they had been endued with the holy spirit, power from on high, which would come at the time of Pentecost. After this, after Pentecost, they were to go forth and teach others. Believers from that time (Pentecost) on *were not to wait or tarry* for the giving of the holy spirit, but they are *to receive* the holy spirit that was given at Pentecost. This promise is for all and to all believers. Acts 2:39 says, "For the promise is unto you, and to your children, and to all that are afar off, *even* as many as the Lord our God shall call." And again we have a direct command in Ephesians 5:18 which admonishes, "And be not drunk with wine, wherein is excess; but be filled with the Spirit [*pneuma*]."

When God's Word gives a direct command, we who are Christ's ought to believe and obey. We also have Paul's clear teaching on this subject. Paul says by revelation in I Corinthians 14:5, "I would that ye all spake with tongues ...." I Corinthians 14:13 tells, "... let him that speaketh in an *unknown* tongue pray [believe] that he may interpret." Paul states in I Corinthians 14:37 that if any man thinks he is a spiritual man, "Let him acknowledge that the things

20

that I write unto you are the commandments of the Lord."

In the Scripture there also are given other reasons why we should receive the holy spirit, namely to have power for Christian service, power for Christian living and power for effective witnessing.

There is potential power in the water of Niagara Falls, but it is unbridled power unless the great dynamos convert it into usable energy. If we use our God-given spiritual abilities, we shall then be effective witnesses of His power from above, as His ability is released by us.

John 16:13-15:
Howbeit when he, the Spirit [the *pneuma*] of truth, is come, he will guide you into all truth: for he shall not speak of himself; but whatsoever he shall hear, *that* shall he speak: and he will shew you things to come.

He shall glorify me: for he shall receive [*lambanō*] of mine, and shall shew *it* unto you.

All things that the Father hath are mine: therefore said I, that he shall take [*lambanō*] of mine, and shall shew *it* unto you.

21

The Holy Spirit will give revelation to those filled with *pneuma hagion*, and so guide into all truth, not half-truth, for it is the whole truth that sets men free.

Jesus' statement to the apostles that the Holy Spirit will "shew you things to come" certainly includes opening up The Word by divine revelation. The statement, "He shall glorify me," means He will enable us to see the glorified Christ more clearly; and if we renew our minds we will become more like Him, we will be formed in the likeness of the Savior as Galatians 4:19 discloses. I John also establishes this truth.

> I John 3:2:
> Beloved, now are we the sons of God, and it doth not yet appear what we shall be: but we know that, when he shall appear, we shall be like him; for we shall see him as he is.

We shall some day, in the glorious coming of the Lord, be like Him. Until that day arrives in the fullness of time, we have the blessed privilege of receiving *pneuma hagion* into manifestation. This power from on high is in us to the end that we may become fashioned in the likeness of our blessed Lord and Savior and Redeemer more and more, day by day.

The Gift from the Holy Spirit

Romans 8:11:
But if the Spirit [*the pneuma*] of him that raised
up Jesus from the dead dwell in you, he that
raised up Christ from the dead shall also quicken
your mortal bodies by his Spirit [*pneuma*] that
dwelleth in you.

Those who have received the holy spirit know this
is true now, and that it will be true on a greater scale
at the time of His coming.

The only way we can gain victory over the carnal
desires of the body and flesh is stated in Romans.

Romans 8:13:
For if ye live after the flesh, ye shall die: but if
ye through the Spirit [*pneuma*] do mortify the
deeds of the body, ye shall live.

After we receive the holy spirit we have the power
from on high in us to help us in our infirmity and our
weakness. The holy spirit helps us in our prayers by
enabling us to pray effectively and by making possible
answered prayers.

Romans 8:26,27:
Likewise the Spirit [the *pneuma*] also helpeth
our infirmities; for we know not what we should
pray for as we ought: but the Spirit [the
pneuma] itself maketh intercession for us with
groanings which cannot be uttered.

And he that searcheth the hearts knoweth what *is* the mind of the Spirit [the *pneuma*], because he maketh intercession for the saints according to *the will of* God.

With all this evidence from the Word of God and with the blessings attending the receiving of the power from on high, no saved person should refuse to manifest the same holy spirit the apostles and disciples received. It thrills my soul to have this wonderful added blessing, and I praise His name that by believing I reached out and received.

CHAPTER TWO

Common Fears that Prevent the Receiving of the Gift from the Holy Spirit

I know what fear can do. I know how Satan can enslave a believer and keep him from receiving the holy spirit into manifestation. I know the common fears which kept me from receiving. And in my dealings with believers, I have discovered that most of them have fears similar to the ones I had.

Most of the fears in regard to receiving the holy spirit into manifestation are due to wrong teaching or ignorance of the Word of God. Our minds have been saturated with thoughts of what others have said and done rather than with what *The Word teaches*. For many people there has been a lack of teaching. Therefore, certain believers do not know that the gift, holy spirit, power from on high, is an indwelling reality in the life of a born-again believer.

Only where there is a clear-cut teaching of the Word of God are fears quickly dispelled for knowledge of The Word roots out fear. I know the terrible spiritual and mental anguish people go through when assailed by fear. I also know the great joy and the overwhelming peace that the believer has when fears are removed by the direct Word of God. We cannot look to God with believing for anything as long as we are beset by fear, for fear builds unbelief, and unbelief defeats the promises of God.

Some people fear that they are going to ask for something which is not for them to receive; they fear that the holy spirit was for the first-century believers only. But Hebrews 13:8 says, "Jesus Christ the same yesterday, and today, and for ever."

This Scripture means what it says — that we may have all that was ever promised or given, and that God's gifts and the manifestations are not limited to the first century. Ephesians 5:18 admonishes, "And be not drunk with wine, wherein is excess; but be filled with the Spirit [*pneuma*]."

This is for all believers, because the book of Ephesians was written to the saints, *believers*, the faithful in Christ Jesus. Thus, Ephesians 5:18 is a definite command from the Word of God that we as believers should be filled. Acts 2:38 stipulates,

"... and ye shall receive the gift of the Holy Ghost [*pneuma hagion*]." The promise then is made to you, as a believer, and to your children as believers and to all believers until the appearing of Jesus Christ or the close of the Church Age.

People have been so frightened by the actions of some who claimed they had received the holy spirit that sincere Christians have denied the reality of the receiving of the holy spirit as a present experience. Good, sincere and honest people in certain religious movements have in many cases "queered" the experience of Pentecost.

I knew that there is such a thing as devil possession and that Satan does supernatural feats. How could I be sure I would not be getting a counterfeit experience when receiving the *pneuma hagion*? This was perhaps my greatest fear.

Luke 11:11-13:
If a son shall ask bread of any of you that is a father, will he give him a stone? or if *he ask* a fish, will he for a fish give him a serpent?

Or if he shall ask an egg, will he offer him a scorpion?

27

If ye then, being evil, know how to give good gifts unto your children: how much more shall *your* heavenly Father give the Holy Spirit [*pneuma hagion*] to them that ask him?

This makes it clear that a human father would not give evil to his son. Then who can possibly believe that our heavenly Father, who loves His children more than any earthly father, would allow a seeking child to be filled with something harmful, wrong or false, when with a deep yearning he is believing to be filled with power from on high according to God's own Word and will?

You may come to God with believing and absolute confidence, knowing that from His hands you receive only good. How dishonoring it is to God when we as children trust our earthly fathers more than our Heavenly Father, thinking that He might allow His hungry children to receive a false or harmful thing when we ask Him for, and believe to receive, the holy spirit into manifestation.

I also feared that I was not good enough to receive power from on high. From a human point of view I knew I was not. I had tried for years to become good enough, but I did not and I could not. The erroneous belief that the holy spirit is given only to those who are good is blocking many people from walking into great deliverance and power. Remember, God gives the gift because we need it, not because we deserve it.

The receiving of any of God's gifts is not in itself a proof of goodness on the part of the receiver. The *pneuma hagion* is *the gift of God.* All gifts of God are received by believing, without any merit on the part of the recipient. God never gives the holy spirit as a reward for living a good, honest life. He gives the *pneuma hagion* to a believer, to do in the believer that which no believer can do in and for himself.

> Romans 10:10:
> For with the heart man believeth unto right-
> eousness; and with the mouth confession is
> made unto salvation.

Righteousness is the spirit from God in man, not the goodness of man. We cannot raise ourselves by our bootstraps to be good enough to receive any of God's gifts. The experience of receiving the power from on high is only the beginning of a fellowship which should lead to the manifestation of victorious living. An added spiritual gift places upon us an added responsibility to manifest this gift in right living. Though someone else fails or neglects to use the gift wisely or properly, we need not be stopped from applying God's best in our lives. Just because one cake fails the housewife does not forever refuse to

29

bake a cake nor does she say all cakes are no good. Just because some may have "queered" the experience of Pentecost, we should not throw overboard the experience of the power from high.

Remember that a gift is a gift. You may give your daughter a beautiful new dress, but she can take your gift and sit down in a mud puddle. She has freedom of will to do this, has she not? But it behooves your daughter to respect your gift and treat it accordingly. So it is with the gift of holy spirit. It behooves the recipient to hold the gift in reverence. We are held accountable for the spiritual light we have and the gifts we possess. A Christian is known in this senses world by the fruit of the spirit he bears, not by the gifts he has or has not received.

The fear of perhaps misusing the holy spirit was another great barrier in my quest. I wanted to be sure that I would not misuse the gift if and when the power came to live in me. Salvation is a gift to us as Ephesians 2:8 tells. As saved believers all will sin; yet, when we confess our sin to God, He reestablishes us in fellowship. We should never purposely want to sin after salvation, after we receive the gift of holy spirit, but if we sin we do not mar the perfection of the gift. We only harm ourselves, and we have God's faithful forgiveness if we confess our sins.

30

I John 1:9:
If we confess our sins, he is faithful and just to forgive us *our* sins, and to cleanse us from all unrightcousness.

All the gifts of God are the means to an end and not ends in themselves. The end is that we might be like Christ. The gift of holy spirit equips us with the ability for a life of greater fruitfulness for God. The power from on high is ours to help us to grow more Christ-like.

The gift of holy spirit is never given on the basis of human merit, but on the basis of grace, as the Bible so clearly teaches. Immediately after receiving the holy spirit, power from on high, a man has no more Christian character than he had the moment before he received, but he now has a source of help and the ability to bring forth spiritual fruit, and this cannot be over-valued.

Galatians 5:22,23:
But the fruit of the Spirit [*pneuma*] is love, joy, peace, longsuffering, gentleness, goodness, faith,

Meekness, temperance: against such there is no law.

Men are known by their *fruit*, and not by the *gifts*

31

they possess. Gifts are no proof of good character. Gifts are received in a moment of time by believing, but producing fruit is growth in disciplined Christian living.

Another fear I had concerned the ability or power Christ said would come upon those who received the holy spirit. Many so-called spirit-filled Christians whom I knew were, by their fruit, indicating ineffective and powerless lives. I could not understand this until one day I realized the difference between a gift and its use. This point may be effectively illustrated. A skillful carpenter has a building site, a set of blueprints and all the materials necessary to build a house according to the plans, but he has no tools whatsoever. In this situation he is unable to build the house. If he is given a chest full of all the tools he needs, he receives the power or ability to build the house. He may, however, sit down on top of the tool chest and fold his hands. It lies within his own power to work or to remain idle. The possession of tools constitutes no guarantee that he will use them. So it is with the one who has received the gift of holy spirit. This believer has power divinely given of God; but he, like the carpenter, may sit down and fold his hands.

Another fear I had was that I might do something foolish before people to make me appear ridiculous and people would say, "He is crazy."

32

Again Luke 11:11-13 came to my attention. God never makes anyone do anything ridiculous or foolish. Every gift of God is a good and perfect gift. Therefore, nothing imperfect comes with God's gift. If some people have, by their actions, demonstrated foolishness, it was not of God but of their own doing. By their own wills they did that which was foolish, for God definitely says in I Corinthians 14:40, "Let all things be done decently and in order." I Corinthians 14:32 says, "And the spirits (*pneumata*) of the prophets are subject to the prophets," which also means that all spiritual abilities from God are subject to the man who receives them. The next verse in I Corinthians also magnifies this truth.

> I Corinthians 14:33:
> For God is not *the author* of confusion, but of peace, as in all churches of the saints.

Man has freedom of will, and his use of the gift is his responsibility. God's gifts *do not possess* people, but people who have God's gifts are responsible for the operation of them.

CHAPTER THREE

Who Is Qualified to Receive the Holy Spirit, Pneuma Hagion?

Most people erroneously believe that a person must be very good to receive the gift of holy spirit, and that only those who have reached an advanced degree of spiritual goodness are qualified. Many people believe that only those who are totally consecrated and disciplined are able to receive. This is as far from the truth as the statement, "You can receive Jesus as your Savior only after you have cleaned up your life." The gift of salvation is by grace and grace alone. Ephesians 2:8 explicitly states, "For by grace are ye saved through faith; and that not of yourselves: *it is* the gift of God."

The gifts of God are never received because of man's good works, nor does God bestow them upon man whenever man reaches a certain spiritual stature. All of God's gifts become man's when he appropriates them by believing, which means the believer acts upon The Word.

The power from on high was given once and for all at Pentecost. This power has been here ever since and is immediately available to anyone who believes to receive. God did all He could on the day of Pentecost; now if man does all he can, he may immediately receive all God gave. All God's gifts are immediately available to every believer. Today it is merely a question of whether or not man wills to receive what God has already given and made available.

There are three things we have to know in order to manifest the more abundant life: we have to know *what* is available to us; we have to know *how* to receive spiritual things; we have to know *what to do* with God's gift after we have received it.

It is a lack of believing on man's part to ask God to send something He has already given. Let me repeat. The gift of God, the gift of holy spirit, is immediately available to anyone who appropriates the gift by believing. The power from on high may be received and manifested by anyone who knows what The Word teaches.

The receiving of the gift from God known as the holy spirit is on the basis of grace and believing. The degrees of spiritual attainment, consecration and personal goodness have no bearing upon receiving the power from on high.

God made an unconditional promise when Jesus Christ said, "I will send you another Comforter." He did not promise that the gift of holy spirit would be given after the apostles reached a certain stage of spiritual development. The Lord knew they needed this added spiritual power in order to be victorious and to be spiritually strong.

Acts 2:38:
Repent, and be baptized every one of you in the name of Jesus Christ for the remission of sins, and ye shall receive the gift of (*from*) the Holy Ghost.

Notice the word "gift." A gift is never earned; wages are. The only righteousness enabling us to receive gifts from God is the righteousness of Christ, which is credited to our spiritual account because of our believing in the one sacrifice of Christ accomplished on the cross.

Most people who desire to receive the gift of holy spirit but who have not, are thoroughly convinced that it is their own fault — that there must be some secret sin or a lack of spirituality preventing their

37

receiving. It is absolutely impossible to receive anything from God as long as you have the idea that you are not good enough to receive. It is like the man who believes he cannot be saved if he sins. If the man concentrates on this thought, he will not believe and be saved; but the moment he is shown what God thinks and what His Word teaches, he may quickly appropriate the gift of salvation by believing.

Another idea which has permeated the thinking of most people searching for the power from on high is that they must wait in prayer as did the apostles before Pentecost. I have heard people say that if a seeker will get in the attitude of prayer as the apostles did ten days before Pentecost, then God will give the seeker the gift of holy spirit. I have seen people spend whole nights and days praying for God to give them the gift of holy spirit, but they have gone away without manifesting, spiritually defeated and wondering what might be wrong in their lives. Why didn't God answer their pleading? Why didn't He give them the holy spirit? God could not give them the power from on high for He had already given it once and for all; but they did not realize that, nor did they know how to receive it.

According to the Bible, the apostles were not instructed to agonize in prayer for ten days to become good enough so that the holy spirit could be given.

38

They were simply instructed to tarry, to wait. For what? For the *fullness of time* for the giving of the gift.

Ten days before the birth of Jesus Christ, those praying for His coming had to wait until the time was fulfilled. The apostles at Pentecost also had to tarry for the appointed time. But since the day of Pentecost there is no tarrying necessary. The waiting and tarrying for the power from on high is over. *It is here.* We need not wait for any gift that God has given. He gave the gift of holy spirit on Pentecost, and the power from on high has been here ever since.

For six years I prayed, asked, pleaded and begged God for this spiritual power. I literally traveled thousands of miles just to ask people about the Holy Spirit and the gift. I always returned spiritually lacerated and bleeding because those Christians who had received were in such confusion that they had no ability to communicate the blessing to me. They were sincere enough, but all they could communicate was experience, and experiences are usually insufficient to lead others into the receiving. They were unable to lead me into an understanding of the Word of God so that I, too, might receive. I almost gave up in despair. But the moment I was made to realize that receiving the holy spirit did not depend upon good works, agonizing in prayer, nor in personal merit, but rather upon believing, that moment I received into manifestation the fullness of the power from on high.

The gift of holy spirit is given that through God's mighty power and by His spiritual help we may grow to be more like Christ. The truth is that a man has no more character, no more ethical goodness immediately after he has received the holy spirit than he had before, but he now has a source of help and power. He has contacted and received the great spiritual force which enables him to build Christian character and to form a more Christ-like life.

This is the age of the Church of the Body under the direction of the Holy Spirit. The Church has lost its first love, its power, its testimony, for Satan has befuddled the mind of man to the extent that the experience of Pentecost has been almost completely unknown to the Church and in the lives of Christians. This is primarily due to a lack of knowledge of the Word of God. The apostles and disciples were the same human beings before and after Pentecost, but something happened that turned them from defeated, fearful, doubting, vacillating men into bold, firm, undaunted apostles and disciples. That something was the receiving of the holy spirit.

Who is qualified to receive the holy spirit? A believer, one who has received Jesus as Lord and believes in his heart that God raised Jesus from the dead.

40

CHAPTER FOUR

What Is Speaking in Tongues?

Speaking in a tongue is the believer's external manifestation in the senses world of the internal reality and presence of the power of the holy spirit. Speaking in tongues is a constant reminder even in the hours of bereavement and sorrow, temptation and trouble, that Christ by way of God's power is in you. Therefore, you have victory over the enemy in every situation because as I John 4:4 states, "... greater is he that is in you, than he that is in the world."

There has been so little clear-cut Biblical teaching about the wonderful blessing of the holy spirit that most people have no idea as to the great value of its manifestation. I will share Biblical teaching with you which will dispel all your fears and, by the help of God, indicate to you what actually occurs when a person speaks in tongues.

Should all born-again believers speak in tongues? In Mark 16:17 Jesus said that believers in His name "... shall speak with new tongues." Notice also the Bible does not say, "Speak in tongues until the death of the original disciples and apostles."

In I Corinthians 14:5 Paul by revelation said, "I would that ye all spake with tongues." Remember that the epistle to the Corinthians was written to the Church. I Corinthians 1:2 stipulates, "Unto the church of God." Thus, it was written to you and me, who are believers, who belong to the Church of the Body. In I Corinthians 14:18 and 37 Paul says, "I thank my God, I speak with tongues more than ye all," and "If any man think himself to be ... spiritual, let him acknowledge that the things that I write unto you are the commandments of the Lord."

Every place in the book of Acts where the holy spirit was received and the initial external manifestation is mentioned, it was always *speaking in tongues*.

Acts 2:4:
... and began to speak with other tongues, as the Spirit [the *pneuma*] gave them utterance.

Acts 10:46:
For they heard them speak with tongues ....

Acts 19:6:
... and they spake with tongues ....

What good does it do to speak in tongues? *It will edify you.* To edify means to build up, to make strong. Where are you edified? Not in your mind because the mind does not understand.

I Corinthians 14:4:
He that speaketh in an *unknown* tongue edifieth himself ....

This manifestation is the only evidence mentioned in the Bible which is specifically for building up the believer in the spirit.

Do you want to be personally edified, built up in the strength of the Lord, and have the power of His might in your life? Then you must speak much in tongues. Of all the spiritual abilities from God, the ability to speak in tongues is the only one the Bible mentions that will build up the believer.

As we eat physical food to strengthen the physical body so we must have spiritual food to build up the spirit. Your mental faculties are not built up through the exercise of speaking in tongues, but your spiritual faculties are greatly strengthened. Things which are in the senses world cannot feed the spirit. This is a law of God.

John 3:6
That which is born of the flesh is flesh; and that which is born of the Spirit is spirit.

This law works with mathematical exactness and scientific precision. Anything that is obtained through the five senses — seeing, hearing, smelling, tasting, touching — is in the senses world and relates itself to the flesh. The Bible is in the senses world, and as such the law of God requires that the Bible feed the mind which is included in the Biblical word "flesh." So if the Bible is in the category of the senses world and thus can feed only the mind, what then will feed the spirit? The only manifestation God ever gave to edify the spirit is speaking in tongues.

When you speak in tongues it is the spirit in you which is in direct communication with your heavenly Father, and as such your spirit is edified. This is the spirit from God in you as a gift which is now your spirit because you have been born again. Could you think of anything more wonderful than a direct communication with God? You have that when you speak in tongues.

I Corinthians 14:2
For he that speaketh in an *unknown* tongue speaketh not unto men, but unto God ....

Notice that you are not speaking unto men when you speak in tongues, but you are speaking unto God. Furthermore, you are speaking *mysteries*.

I Corinthians 14:2:
... howbeit in the spirit he speaketh mysteries.

This word "mysteries" may be translated "divine secrets." Imagine any believer refusing something whereby he, by the spirit, may speak divine secrets directly with God. Those who know the Biblical teaching and in their own private life speak much in tongues are greatly edified and built up in the spirit with mighty boldness. They become spiritually keen and spiritually perceptive.

When you pray in the spirit, which is praying in tongues, you may rest assured that there is no selfishness in your prayer, for your understanding is bypassed; such prayer is a direct spiritual communication with the Father. When we pray with our understanding, selfishness may enter and then we pray amiss, but we never pray amiss when we pray by or through the spirit.

I Corinthians 14:14,15:
For if I pray in an *unknown* tongue, my spirit prayeth, but my understanding is unfruitful.

What is it then? I will pray with the spirit, and I will pray with the understanding also: I will sing with the spirit, and I will sing with the understanding also.

I have awakened many times during the night feeling a great burden to pray, but as I did not know by my senses what I should pray for or about, I just prayed the best I could. Seemingly there are people or situations in the world which God would have believers pray for; but unless we pray in tongues, the prayer is not offered nor the burden lifted. Since receiving into manifestation the holy spirit and praying in tongues in my private prayer life, I have learned that when these prayer burdens come and I pray to the Father in tongues as the Spirit gives utterance, the burden soon lifts and my prayer is heard and answered. This has been demonstrated numerous times for very sick people, for people in trouble or in grave danger. I firmly believe that God would have us pray for many things which the human mind overlooks. Since the Holy Spirit directs what is prayed in tongues, we can pray for the fulfillment of specific needs unknown to our senses minds.

Another wonderful asset of speaking in tongues is that we are helped in overcoming our infirmities. Which believer among us has no infirmity to overcome or weakness for which he needs help?

Romans 8:26,27:
Likewise the Spirit [the *pneuma*] also helpeth our infirmities:* for we know not what we should pray for as we ought: but the Spirit [the *pneuma*] itself maketh intercession for us with groanings which cannot be uttered.

*In the original text, "infirmity" is singular — the infirmity is that sense-knowledgewise "we know not what we should pray for as we ought."

46

And he that searcheth the hearts knoweth what *is* the mind of the Spirit, because he maketh intercession for the saints according to *the will of* God.

Why speak in tongues if the one speaking cannot understand what is spoken? Isn't that foolish and silly? Nothing is foolish and silly which is commanded by God and carried out according to God's plan and order. You do not think it foolish to breathe even though you cannot see the air; nor do you think it foolish to flip the electric switch simply because you cannot see the electricity. You will no longer think it is jabbering or foolishness when you speak in tongues once you have received the power from on high into manifestation. Then, and not before, you will realize what light and life it brings to you.

Now I want to clarify for you the second most misunderstood portion of the Bible relating to the whole subject of speaking in tongues.

How does one speak in tongues?

No one speaks in tongues until after he is born again and the holy spirit is permanently within. Devils *cannot* speak in tongues. Thus, when one speaks in tongues one can never speak devilish or wrong things.* Devils can possess people to

*See chapter XIV, page 114, answer to Question No. 8.

47

prophesy, but devils never speak in tongues.* Those who teach that devils can inspire one to speak in tongues have been misled. Every verse in the Bible dealing with speaking in tongues says that the speakers glorified God. I have included this paragraph here because I firmly believe we have to base all teaching on the Bible and not on what men may say. Speaking in tongues, as I said in the first paragraph of this chapter, is the external manifestation of the internal reality and presence of the *gift* of holy spirit from the *Giver* who is the Holy Spirit.

The gifts of God throughout the Bible are received by believing, and all are operated by direct action of the human will. The Spirit does not do the speaking. *We do the speaking, but what we speak is the Holy Spirit's choosing.*

If we do the speaking we can stop at will and start at will. We have complete control over the speaking in tongues at all times even as we have control over speaking with our understanding. When

---

*Jeremiah 2:8: "... and the prophets prophesied by Baal, and walked after *things that* do not profit."
I Kings 18:19: "Now therefore send, *and* gather to me all Israel unto mount Carmel, and the prophets of Baal four hundred and fifty, and the prophets of the groves four hundred, which eat at Jezebel's table."
Ezekiel 13.17: "Likewise, thou son of man, set thy face against the daughters of thy people, which prophesy out of their own heart; and prophesy thou against them."

we speak in tongues, however, we have no jurisdiction
over the language we may be speaking.

Acts 2:4:
And they were all filled with the Holy Ghost
[*pneuma hagion*], and [they, not the spirit]
began to speak with other tongues, as the Spirit
[the *pneuma*] gave them utterance.

They were all filled and began to speak. Who began
to speak? *They did.* Did the Holy Spirit do the
speaking? No! *The ones who were filled did.* If they
did the speaking, then they controlled the speaking;
but *what* they spoke was "as the Spirit gave them
utterance." The Holy Spirit *never* does the speaking.
The Bible plainly teaches that man by *his own will*
does the speaking, but what is spoken is super-
naturally directed.

Speaking in tongues by a born-again believer is absolutely based on an act of the human will. There is
nothing supernatural about the fact that man may
speak in tongues. Man's will is always in control, but
the supernatural involved in the whole operation is
what he speaks and not the fact *that* he speaks.

The Holy Spirit *never* possesses a man or forces
him to speak against his will. There is not one verse of
Scripture in the Bible that teaches that God takes

possession of man's will. Man may say God possesses, but that does not make it so.

If man had no control over speaking in tongues, then God would have transgressed one of His own laws — man's freedom of will — which God cannot and will not do. Furthermore, it would be foolish for the Bible to have such clear teaching, as *when* to speak and *when not* to speak in tongues, if believers were unable to carry out the instructions set forth.

> I Corinthians 14:14,15:
> For if I pray in an *unknown* tongue, my spirit [*pneuma*] prayeth, but my understanding is unfruitful.
> What is it then? I will pray with the spirit [the *pneuma*], and I will pray with the understanding also: I will sing with the spirit [the *pneuma*], and I will sing with the understanding also.

Notice carefully that Paul says, "For if I pray in an *unknown* tongue, my spirit prayeth." Who is praying? Paul is doing the praying, not the Holy Spirit. Paul says he can by his own will pray in tongues. He wills, by his own decision, to pray not only "with the spirit," which is praying in tongues, but "with the understanding," which is praying with the senses. We, by our own wills, determine to pray with the understanding and, likewise, we, by our own wills, determine to pray with the spirit.

50

What Is Speaking in Tongues?

Do not let *anyone* ever tell you again that the Holy Spirit does the speaking or praying. The Bible clearly teaches that we by our wills speak in tongues. This discards the negative ideas and thoughts and the wrong teaching that we have no control over speaking in tongues. We are *always* in perfect control of every spiritual gift of God. Every spiritual ability, gift of the true God, is operated by our decision. If it *ever* appears that a spiritual manifestation is out of control, it is in reality not the manifestation which is out of control, but rather the man operating the manifestation is out of order. When this occurs it is not a glory to God, nor is it edifying to the household of faith, but it is a misuse of something intended for good.

All gifts are received by believing. Since it is impossible to speak two languages at the same time, the position of believing in receiving into manifestation the holy spirit is that the believer will receive *lambanō*, manifest the power from on high, and at that very moment expect a supernatural movement of the spiritual ability within him. Jesus spoke of this experience of the spirit.

John 7:38,39:

He that believeth on me, as the scripture hath said, out of his belly shall flow rivers of living water.

(But this spake he of the Spirit [the *pneuma*],

51

which they that believe on him should receive:
for the Holy Ghost [*pneuma hagion*] was not
yet *given*; because that Jesus was not yet
glorified).

Man's next step in believing is to lift his voice and
boldly speak forth. The spirit has no organs of
speech. Therefore, we must move our lips and make
the sounds and speak the words, but the sounds and
the words we speak are God's doing. We, by our wills,
speak forth. This is our believing, our action. The *act*
of speaking is *our* doing, but *what* we speak is God's
part of the manifestation.

Speaking in tongues is not:

1. Linguistic ability. It is an inspired expression of
a language which may or may not be understood by
people somewhere in the world. (I Corinthians 13:1)

2. The gift of known languages nor the com-
prehension of languages.

3. Yelling, shouting nor making hideous jabbering
noises.

*Speaking in tongues is the God-given spiritual
ability to speak in other tongues at will as the Spirit
gives utterance.* We can start any time; we can stop
any time. By our wills we are always in absolute and
perfect control of speaking in tongues.

What Is Speaking in Tongues?

Speaking in tongues is for:

1. Our private prayer life, first and foremost. When used in the Church, speaking in tongues *must be* accompanied by interpretation. (I Corinthians 14:4,5)

2. Edification of our spirit, our new creation in Christ Jesus. (I Corinthians 14:4)

3. Communications with God in "mysteries" or "divine secrets." (I Corinthians 14:2)

4. The giving of thanks well. (I Corinthians 14:17)

5. Keeping us aware that we are God's children and joint-heirs with Christ. (Romans 8:16)

6. Helping us to overcome our infirmity. (Romans 8:26)

7. Helping us to pray aright. (Romans 8:26)

8. Making intercession with God for us as individual believers. (Romans 8:26, 27)

9. Making intercession with God for the saints, the other believers, the Church. (Romans 8:27)

10. Strengthening us with His might in the inner man. (Ephesians 3:16)

CHAPTER FIVE

How to Receive the Holy Spirit, Pneuma Hagion

Before we can receive anything from God we must first be sure that it is God's will for us to have it. If we are not sure that God wants us to have the holy spirit, we cannot receive, for then we are not certain that the power is available. Thus, *we must know the Word of God before we can do the will of God.*

Furthermore, we must be rid of all fear regarding the holy spirit and speaking in tongues. No one with fear can believe; and without believing, it is impossible to receive any of God's gifts. All spiritual gifts are received and operated in the individual by believing.

If you have a deep spiritual hunger to receive into manifestation the power from on high and to have the ability that you read about in the book of Acts and throughout the entire New Testament, you may receive that power while reading this chapter. It is possible to receive the holy spirit at any moment after we know what God has made available and know how to receive it. God's gift of holy spirit has been given once and for all, and you need not tarry to receive it. *Only believe.*

Let us note the general order for the receiving of this power from on high for the Church Age as set forth in God's Word by Peter in his great sermon shortly after the giving of the holy spirit on the day of Pentecost.

Acts 2:38:

Then Peter said unto them, Repent, and be baptized every one of you in the name of Jesus Christ for the remission of sins, and ye shall receive the gift of the Holy Ghost [the *pneuma hagion*].

The particularly important statement to us is, "Ye shall receive the gift of the Holy Ghost." A gift is something which cannot be earned or worked for because the moment we begin to work for it, it ceases to be a gift and becomes wages or a reward for labor. If we get anything because we have done something good or virtuous, then it is a reward for merit. The giving of power from on high was another demonstration of the grace of God and not a reward for achievement. He freely gives, not because we are worthy but because of His loving kindness and our great need. We are no more worthy to receive the holy spirit, than we are worthy to receive any other of God's gifts. All are gracious gifts to needy persons from a loving God.

Luke 11:13:
If ye then, being evil, know how to give good gifts unto your children: how much more shall *your* heavenly Father give the Holy Spirit [*pneuma hagion*] to them that ask him?

In The Word, receiving the holy spirit is on a gift basis. Here Luke says your Father will give. This was spoken before Pentecost. *After Pentecost the idea of giving the holy spirit is never once mentioned.* God, the Holy Spirit, gave the gift, *pneuma hagion,* holy spirit, once and for all at Pentecost. From then on, it has been a matter of man's receiving by believing.

Do you want to receive? It is no longer a question of God's doing His part; He has done it. It is now a question of your doing your part to receive.

The word "receive" applies to action on the part of the one who desires to get something. Since speaking in an unknown tongue is the initial outward manifestation of the internal reality and presence of the holy spirit, we should expect to speak another tongue immediately upon receiving the holy spirit. Since we

57

cannot speak two languages at once, we must lay aside all thought of speaking words in a language which we know and operate by our understanding. We speak forth an inspired language by believing.

We cannot make a mistake in our quest. Remember I Samuel 16.

> I Samuel 16:7:
> But the Lord said unto Samuel, Look not on his countenance, or on the height of his stature; because I have refused him: for *the Lord seeth* not as man seeth; for man looketh on the outward appearance, but the Lord looketh on the heart.

We cannot be wrong in God's sight as long as we believe rightly. He will withhold no good thing from His seeking and believing children.

Remember that the Holy Spirit is God, and that He has made it possible for His gift, holy spirit, to dwell in us. God sent the holy spirit as a loving and gracious gift to His people, not because we are worthy, or deserve or merit it, but because we are hungry and desperately need spiritual abilities to wage a good warfare and to run the race of life with power — His ability.

> Galatians 3:5:
> He therefore that ministereth to you the Spirit

[the *pneuma*], and worketh miracles among you, *doeth he it* by the works of the law, or by the hearing of faith?

I want you particularly to notice the words "ministereth to you." When I teach an audience, I "minister" The Word to them, I give out The Word.

Acts 8:18:
And when Simon saw that through laying on of the apostles' hands the Holy Ghost [*pneuma hagion*] was given, he offered them money.

The holy spirit may be ministered directly and with absolute certainty. I have ministered the holy spirit many times to men and women from various denominational backgrounds, and never have I seen a failure if the candidate believes to receive. When a candidate is instructed and understands that the Word of God is the Will of God and he acts accordingly, there can be no failure.

People have said to me, "Yes, I know the apostles could and did minister the holy spirit, but who are you?" Then I remind them that I, as a born-again believer filled with God's power, am a steward of the manifold grace of God, and I minister with the ability that God has given me.* Ananias, who ministered the holy spirit to Saul of Tarsus, was also just a believer.

I know that the holy spirit can be received into manifestation without the presence of any other person or without the laying on of hands but *never* without believing.

I instruct people to receive the holy spirit in the following manner. It is only a method, but God has blessed it and people have received thereby.

1. Get quiet and relaxed. "Be still and know that I am God." The greatest cargoes of life come in on quiet seas.

2. Do not beg God for the holy spirit. It is here. The power has been here ever since Pentecost. There is no waiting and no tarrying necessary.

3. Rest your head back and breathe in deeply. The word "inspiration" also means "in-breathing."

By believing, you can breathe in the spirit. Opening your mouth and breathing in deeply is an act of believing which God honors.

I Peter 4:10,11: "As every man hath received the gift, *even so* minister the same one to another, as good stewards of the manifold grace of God. If any man speak, *let him speak* as the oracles of God; if any man minister, *let him do it* as of the ability which God giveth: that God in all things may be glorified through Jesus Christ, to whom be praise and dominion for ever and ever. Amen."

Psalms 81:10:
... open thy mouth wide, and I will fill it.

Psalms 119:131:
I opened my mouth, and panted: for I longed for thy commandments.

The Greek text of Acts 2:2, "as of a rushing mighty wind," should be translated "as of a heavy breathing." Relaxation and in-breathing are vital keys to receiving the holy spirit into manifestation. In John 7, Jesus specifically tells us to drink in the holy spirit.

John 7:37–39:
... If any man thirst, let him come unto me, and drink.

He that believeth on me, as the scripture hath said, out of his belly shall flow rivers of living water.

(But this spake he of the Spirit [*pneuma*], which they that believe on him should receive: for the Holy Ghost [*pneuma*] was not yet *given*; because that Jesus was not yet glorified.)

In Job 29:23 we read, "And they opened their mouth wide *as* for the latter rain." We must open our mouths to drink. This is a helpful step toward receiving into manifestation the spiritual power from on high. If you will do this, you shall realize the manifestation.

In the Gospel of John, Jesus gave last-minute instructions to His apostles before His ascension.

John 20:22:
And when he had said this, he breathed on [*en*, in; He breathed in.] *them* [delete], and saith unto them, Receive [*lambanō*] ye the Holy Ghost [*pneuma hagion*].

Since the holy spirit, the power from on high, was not given until Pentecost, they could not have received it at that time. Therefore, "Receive ye" meant later, on the day of Pentecost.

4. Finally, pray this prayer: "Father, I now receive the holy spirit, the power from on high, which you made available through Jesus Christ."

Having carried out these four simple steps to receiving the power of the holy spirit, you must now by your own will, move your lips, your tongue, your throat; you must make the sounds, form the words. But the words that you speak will be as "the Spirit giveth utterance." *What* you speak is God's business; but *that* you speak is your business.

SECTION TWO

The book of Acts has five accounts of receiving the gift from the Holy Spirit either by individuals or groups. These five records are progressive in reception, and they contain all the information necessary to receive the gift from the Holy Spirit. We will now study each of these records in detail.

CHAPTER SIX

A Study of Acts 1 and 2

Before we study the record in Acts 2, which is the original outpouring of the gift from the Holy Spirit, we must endeavor to understand three things; namely, what it was that came on the day of Pentecost, where it occurred and who was present to receive.

We shall first of all set ourselves to the task of discovering exactly what it was that came on the day of Pentecost.

Acts 1:4:
And, being assembled together with *them,* [Jesus] commanded them that they should not depart from Jerusalem, but wait for the promise of the Father, which, *saith he*, ye have heard of me.

The time of this verse is the day of the ascension, which was forty days from the resurrection when Jesus was gathered together with His apostles and was giving them last-minute instructions before His departure. He instructed them, as a matter of fact He commanded them, that they should not depart from Jerusalem, but were to wait for the promise of the Father.

You and I, looking back, know that Pentecost was ten days after the ascension, but the apostles looking ahead did not know exactly when this promise of the Father was to be fulfilled. Therefore, they were instructed to wait or tarry.

What were they to wait for? The Word of God said they were to "wait for the promise of the Father which ... ye have heard of me."

In Acts we read about the baptism of the Holy Spirit.

Acts 1:5:
For John truly baptized with water; but ye shall be baptized with [the Greek word is *en*, the equivalent of "in"] the Holy Ghost [*pneuma hagion*] not many days hence.

Thus, whatever it is to be baptized in *pneuma*

hagion, holy spirit, equals whatever the promise of the Father is. Or, turning it around, "the promise of the Father," in verse 4 equals whatever it is to be "baptized in *pneuma hagion.*"

The reason Jesus commanded the apostles to wait was that the gift had not yet been given. If you were instructed that next Tuesday you were to receive a gift from a very dear friend, then it would be necessary for you to wait until next Tuesday because the present would not be available until then. So it was with the receiving of the holy spirit.

We know from the Word of God that after the gift was once given on the day of Pentecost, which was ten days after the ascension, there are no instructions for anyone to wait or tarry to receive the gift. The teaching that we, in this day and age, must tarry to receive any of God's gifts is contrary to the Word of God. For example, salvation is a gift and it is immediately available. We need not tarry to be saved because salvation is a present obtainable reality.

The Gospel of Luke, which was written by the same person who wrote the book of Acts, reads in chapter 24, verse 49, "And, behold, I send the promise of my Father upon you: but tarry ye in the city of Jerusalem, until ye be endued with power from on high." In Acts the apostles were told not to depart from Jerusalem but to "wait for the promise of the Father, which ... ye have heard of me." In verse 5 of Acts 1, Jesus said, "Ye shall be baptized with the Holy Ghost not many days hence." From these Scripture verses it is clear that "the promise of the Father" and the power with which they were to be "endued ... from on high," were referring to the same thing – the baptism with *pneuma hagion*, holy spirit.

The mathematical axiom, "things equal to the same thing are equal to each other" is applicable here:

the promise of the Father (Acts 1:4)

equals

to be baptized with *pneuma hagion* (Acts 1:5)

equals

endued with power from on high (Luke 24:49).

The word "endued" is "clothed with" or "arrayed with." "Power" is the Greek word *dunamis.* It is not automatically manifested power; it is inherent power. They were to be endued with power from on high.

Three verses take all the guesswork out of what came on the day of Pentecost. It could not be the Holy Spirit because the Holy Spirit is God. He has been from the beginning and He is the Giver; He gives that which He is. God is *pneuma,* Spirit; God is *hagion,* Holy. Therefore, giving what He is, His gift on the day of Pentecost was *pneuma hagion* which is explained in Luke 24:49, to be "endued with power from on high." This is vitally informative and instructive. It tells us exactly what it is to be baptized with holy spirit. It is to be clothed, not externally but internally, with *dunamis,* inherent power. This power is His power, which is spirit. The Word tells us where it came from — "on high," namely, from God. Thus, these three verses, two from Acts and one from Luke, put together the great accuracy of the Word of God as to exactly what was received on Pentecost and is described in the second chapter of Acts. There is no room left for private interpretation as to what was given. These verses of Scripture reveal all that can be known.

Reading on in Luke 24, we see that Jesus led the apostles to Bethany.

Luke 24:50-52:
... he lifted up his hands, and blessed them.

69

And it came to pass, while he blessed them, he was parted from them, and carried up into heaven.

And they worshipped him, and returned to Jerusalem with great joy.

The apostles carried out literally the instructions of their Lord and Savior in returning to Jerusalem to tarry until they would be "endued with power from on high," which is "the promise of the Father," which is to be "baptized with [*pneuma hagion*] holy spirit."

Returning to Acts 1, we read the instruction that Jesus gave to the apostles.

Acts 1:8
But ye shall receive [*lambano*, to receive into manifestation] power [*dunamis*, inherent power], after [or when] that the Holy Ghost [the *hagion pneuma*] is come upon you: and ye shall be witnesses unto me both in Jerusalem, and in all Judaea, and in Samaria, and unto the uttermost part of the earth.

Jesus instructed the apostles to wait until they were endued with power from on high, and then they were to show forth this power, *lambano* it. No one can show spiritual power in the senses world until he has first received it spiritually. In other words, a person must be saved, born again of God's Spirit, filled with the power from the Holy Spirit, before he can manifest forth the evidence of the holy spirit in the world of the senses. Jesus said that after, or when, they received this power from on high, then they were to be witnesses unto Him. This is a tremendous truth. The apostles were not to be defense attorneys. They were to be witnesses.*

When you have truth, you need not defend it, all you need to do is to witness to it. There is no apologizing for or qualifying of truth. It is when you do not have truth that you have to argue about it and endeavor to defend it.

Those who are born again of God's Spirit and are filled with the power of the holy spirit are to be witnesses. This is the instruction the Lord gave to His apostles shortly before He was received up into heaven. They were to be witnesses unto Him in Jerusalem, in Judea, in Samaria and unto the uttermost part of the earth, and certainly the uttermost part of the earth includes the places where you and I live today.

*They were witnesses unto Him by their speaking in tongues. Acts 2:4: "And they were all filled with the Holy Ghost, and began to speak with other tongues, as the Spirit gave them utterance."

Acts 1:9 — 13:
And when he had spoken these things, while
they beheld, he was taken up; and a cloud
received him out of their sight.

And while they looked stedfastly toward heaven
as he went up, behold, two men stood by them
in white apparel;

Which also said, Ye men of Galilee [Note very
carefully "men of Galilee." Of the twelve
apostles only Judas was a Judean, all the rest
were Galileans.*], why stand ye gazing up into
heaven? this same Jesus, which is taken up from
you into heaven, shall so come in like manner as
ye have seen him go into heaven.

Then returned they [the men of Galilee, the
eleven apostles] unto Jerusalem from the mount
called Olivet, which is from Jerusalem a sabbath
day's journey.

And when they [the apostles] were come in
[into Jerusalem], they [the apostles] went up
into an upper room, where abode both Peter,
and James, and John, and Andrew, Philip, and

*Victor Paul Wierwille, *The Bible Tells Me So — Volume I, Studies in
Abundant Living* (American Christian Press, New Knoxville, Ohio,
1971), Chapter 16, "When Judas Hanged Himself."

Thomas, Bartholomew, and Matthew, James *the son* of Alphaeus, and Simon Zelotes, and Judas *the brother* of James.

These are tremendously important verses. They inform us that the upper room was a place where the apostles abode. In other words, this was a place where they stayed, where they slept. In the Eastern land of Biblical history, no woman is ever allowed in the sleeping quarters of men; nor would a man be allowed in the sleeping quarters of a woman. Even the cleaning of the upper room would be in the hands of a male servant. The Bible specifically says that the upper room was the place where the apostles abode. This is where they slept. This is where they stayed overnight.

I want you to remember that it is not the day of Pentecost about which the Word of God is speaking in Acts 1:13. It is speaking about the day of the ascension. On that day the apostles returned to the upper room where they lived, and there they stayed as they were waiting or tarrying for "the promise of the Father," which equals being "baptized with *pneuma hagion*," which is equivalent to being "endued with power from on high." This was to take place "not many days hence." During those days, the days of waiting, the apostles used the upper room as their living quarters.

The next verse is a record in the Word of God of events between the day of the ascension and the day of Pentecost.

> Acts 1:14:
> These all [all the eleven] continued with one accord [with unity of purpose] in prayer and supplication, with the women, and Mary the mother of Jesus, and with his brethren.

It does not say that these all continued with one accord in prayer and supplication in the upper room. It could not have been the upper room because women were present. Where could this possibly have happened?

Turning to Luke 24:53, we have evidence of the location of the outpouring of the gift. Here it says regarding the apostles that they "were continually in the temple, praising and blessing God." How could they be continually in the temple and still be in the upper room? Some people have said that this is a contradiction, but it is not. The Word of God says that they were *continually* in the Temple. It does not say they were there continuously. "Continually" means that they were periodically in the Temple, when they were supposed to be there. When were they supposed to be there? At the hours of prayer. What were the hours of prayer? These we know from

74

the Old Testament record as well as from the modern customs of the Jews and also the Mohammedans. There are five hours of prayer referred to in the Bible, roughly corresponding to our 6 A.M., 9 A.M., 12 Noon, 3 P.M. and 6 P.M.

The full account of the outpouring of the gift from the Holy Spirit on the day of Pentecost is recorded in Acts 2:1-13. Verses 14-47 of the same chapter record what Peter said to the assembled multitude by way of explanation of what had happened. The beginning of Peter's speech, as given in verse 15, establishes the exact hour marking the climax of the outpouring: "These are not drunken, as ye suppose, seeing it is *but* the third hour of the day." The third hour of the day was an hour of prayer, corresponding to our 9 A.M.

Where was the gift from the Holy Spirit poured out? Not in the upper room, because the upper room was the living quarters of the apostles, but in the Temple, the house of God, the place where they were "continually" at the hours of prayer. This documentation of the "third hour of the day" gives us the exact time, as well as the place, where the gift from the Holy Spirit was received. No private interpretation can change the truth as it is clearly recorded in the Scripture.

Sometime between the first and the third hours, on

the day of Pentecost, the outpouring of the gift from the Holy Spirit occurred exactly as it is recorded in Acts 2:1—4. The first and third hours of the day were hours of prayer when the apostles would not have been in the upper room, but in the Temple.

The reason we have all believed that Pentecost happened in the upper room is that we have been wrongly taught. I believe that we were taught this because of the words "the house" used in Acts 2:2. Read this passage carefully and note that it does not say that it filled all the upper room where they were sitting. It specifically states that "it filled all the house where they were sitting." Jesus Christ Himself spoke of the Temple as "the house," "His house"; in Luke 19:46, He said, "My house is the house of prayer ...." This last statement re-echoes the writing of the prophet Isaiah in which the Lord called His house a house of prayer.

> Isaiah 56:7:
> Even them will I bring to my holy mountain, and make them joyful in my house of prayer: their burnt offerings and their sacrifices *shall be* accepted upon mine altar; for mine house shall be called an house of prayer for all people.

God had promised through the years that He

would meet His people in the Temple; and so on the day of Pentecost He came to His house and gave His gift of *pneuma hagion* to the waiting apostles. This news, according to Acts 2:6, was "noised abroad," and a multitude assembled to see and hear what was happening. The upper room could not have accommodated a multitude, but a multitude could assemble in the Temple, the house of prayer.

For those of us who sincerely believe God's Word is God's Will, and that it means what it says and says what it means, there can be no doubt as to the time and the place of the happening of Pentecost.

Before we specifically consider the verses in Acts 2, word by word and line by line, we must pursue one further observation from the Word of God. We yet need to know who and how many were present to receive the outpouring at Pentecost.

To document this truth we must return to Acts 1:15 where we read, "And in those days ...." What days? The days between the ascension and Pentecost while the apostles were tarrying for the promise of the Father.

Acts 1:15:
And in those days Peter stood up in the midst of the disciples, and said, (the number of names together were about an hundred and twenty,)

"In those days," before the day of Pentecost, Peter stood up and "... the names together were about an hundred and twenty." This specifically says that Peter stood up here during the interim between the ascension and Pentecost, and at that time there were "... about an hundred and twenty." The significance of this to any Bible student who sincerely wants to rightly divide and understand the Word of God is astounding. On one of those days, before the outpouring, when there were about one hundred and twenty present, Peter spoke to them concerning the selection of one of their number to replace Judas as one of the twelve apostles. This was in fulfillment of the Scripture. After they had prayed, according to Acts 1:26, "they gave forth their lots; and the lot fell upon Matthias; and he was numbered with the eleven apostles." Reading on to the next verse which is Acts 2:1 the first word is "and," which is a conjunction tying together Matthias with the eleven apostles, with whom he was numbered. "And when the day of Pentecost was fully come they ...." "They" who? "They" is a pronoun and it relates itself to its closest associated noun which is the eleven apostles and Matthias who was numbered with them.

There is no record in the Bible stating that there were one hundred and twenty gathered in the upper room on the day of Pentecost waiting to receive the gift from the Holy Spirit. This is highly significant to

78

an understanding of the events that took place at the outpouring from the Holy Spirit.

Acts 2:1 – 4:
And when the day of Pentecost was fully come, they [the twelve apostles] were all with one accord in one place [the Temple].

And suddenly there came a sound from heaven as of a rushing mighty wind, and it filled all the house [the Temple] where they [the twelve apostles] were sitting.

And there appeared unto them [the twelve apostles] cloven tongues like as of fire, and it sat upon each of them.

And they [the twelve apostles] were all filled with the Holy Ghost [*pneuma hagion*], and began to speak with other tongues, as the Spirit [the *pneuma*] gave them utterance.

On the occasion of the outpouring on the day of Pentecost, only the twelve apostles received into manifestation the gift from the Holy Spirit. In verses 6 and 7 we have the record of a multitude coming together to see and hear what was happening.

79

Acts 2:6,7:
Now when this was noised abroad, the multitude came together, and were confounded, because that every man heard them speak in his own language.

And they were all amazed and marvelled, saying one to another, Behold, are not all these which speak Galilaeans?

This is further proof that only the twelve apostles received the gift, because not all of the disciples who made up the group of about one hundred and twenty would necessarily be Galileans; but Matthias and the eleven other apostles were Galileans. Verse 14 adds more light and insight.

Acts 2:14:
But Peter, standing up with the eleven ....

This agrees with the record that Matthias was numbered with the eleven apostles, making twelve. The pronouns "they" and "them" appearing in Acts 2:1,2,3 and 4 refer to the twelve.

There is no doubt, there is no question, there is no argument as to *what* was given on the day of Pentecost — *pneuma hagion*, power from on high — nor as to *where* the outpouring from the Holy Spirit took

80

place – in the Temple; nor is there any question about *who* received the outpouring at Pentecost, namely, the twelve apostles. This removes the guesswork and simply allows the Word of God to be the Will of God, for it says what it means and means what it says.

We are now ready to read accurately the record in the first four verses of Acts 2.

Acts 2:1
And when the day of Pentecost was fully come, they [the twelve apostles] were all with one accord in one place [the Temple].

The outpouring of the gift from the Holy Spirit on Pentecost had been in the process of coming ever since the fall of man recorded in Genesis 3, but it never "fully came" until the day of Pentecost. All through the Old Testament we see various manifestations from the Spirit in operation, and we see the order of God's program bringing to pass the coming of the power from the Holy Spirit; but the gift never *fully came* until Pentecost about which we are reading in Acts 2. On this day the twelve apostles were in the Temple because it was an hour of prayer, and they were all in one accord: they were all with unity of purpose; they were praying.

Verse 2:
And suddenly there came a sound from heaven as of a rushing mighty wind ....

The word "heaven" is used in the Bible as meaning any place above the earth. The sound "as of a rushing mighty wind" therefore came from above the earth. One translator has translated it much more accurately as, "There came a sound from heaven as of a hard [or heavy] breathing."*

This agrees with what Jesus told the apostles as recorded in the Gospel of John before the day of the ascension.

John 20:22:
And when he had said this, he breathed on *them* [he breathed in], and saith unto them, Receive ye the Holy Ghost [*pneuma hagion*].

Could the disciples have received the gift from the Holy Spirit at that time? No, for it was before Pentecost when Jesus spoke this. And there is an absolute law in operation for the spiritual world as well as in the natural world, namely, that no one can receive *anything* until it is available. The power from

*A New Translation from the Revised Text of the Greek Original, Second Edition, Revised. London: G. Morrish, 24, Warwith Lane, Paternoster Row, E.C. *Pnoēs,* is not "wind," but "as of a hard breathing."

the Holy Spirit or the gift from the Holy Spirit was not available until the day of Pentecost, otherwise Jesus would not have needed to tell them to tarry or wait. Then what was Jesus doing according to John 20:22? He was instructing His disciples: "... he breathed on *them* [He breathed in] ...." He was telling them what to do when the time came; they were to breathe in heavily at the proper moment.

Acts 2:2:
... and it filled [What filled? This heavy breathing by the apostles] all the house, [the Temple] where they were sitting.

The apostles in the Temple were in the posture common to the hour of prayer. They were not shouting; they were neither making loud noises nor pleading and begging God. They were sitting. Please be reminded that the Word of God says, "they were sitting." In other words, they were decent and in order as all things must be if they are to agree with the accuracy of God's Word. However, posture has nothing to do with receiving anything from God. Spiritual gifts do not depend upon man-made forms or customs. We receive from God because of our believing.

Verse 3:
And there appeared unto them [the twelve

apostles] cloven tongues like as of fire, and it sat upon each of them.

It does not say that the cloven tongues *were fire*, but they appeared *like fire*. "Cloven tongues like as of fire" is the phenomenon which occurred on the day of Pentecost.

The difference between *phenomena* and that which the Word of God *guarantees* to everyone must be understood. What God has promised in His Word He is not only *able* to perform, but He *will* perform whenever a person believes. In other words, every promise in the Word of God is readily available and accessible to every believer at the time he believes. This is guaranteed. God cannot break His Word when we believe. Nothing is a phenomenon which is guaranteed in the Word of God and made available to anyone and everyone who wills to believe. God is no respecter of persons, but of conditions only. When we fulfill the conditions, His Word being His Will comes into manifestation.

But God, being Almighty, can go beyond His Word in dealing with people. Whenever and wherever God goes beyond what is guaranteed in His Word to a believer, such manifestations are phenomena. But those occurrences which go beyond the guarantee cannot contradict His revealed Word. Upon those occasions in the Word of God, and only those occasions when

84

God goes beyond that which is guaranteed to everyone, it is a phenomenon.

For example, the writing on the wall at the time of Belshazzar's feast was a phenomenon, because it is not guaranteed in the Word of God that every time a wicked king has a feast there will be messages written on the wall. It is God's prerogative to give any man or any believer phenomena if He so desires. But He cannot do less than His Word when a man believes. God can do more, and, if and when He does more for any individual, it is always a phenomenon.

The phenomenon on the day of Pentecost was that "there appeared unto them [the twelve apostles] cloven tongues like as of fire." "The cloven tongues like as of fire" is not guaranteed to every believer; therefore, it is a phenomenon. This truth which I have set before you will fit every phenomenal presentation of God throughout the entire Word of God.

The "cloven tongues like as of fire ... sat upon each of them." The word "sat" is especially interesting. As we study the Word of God, we discover that on a number of occasions when something was finished, totally completed, the word "sat" is used. For instance, after the six days of creation Genesis 2:2 says, "And he [God] rested [sat]." God's creative activity was completely finished. After Jesus Christ had given His life, was raised again and ascended into heaven, He "sat down on the right hand of God," as Hebrews 10:12 records. When man's redemption was completed, Jesus Christ "sat down."

On the day of Pentecost the gift from the Holy Spirit was "fully come." That is why Acts 2:3 states, "... and it sat upon each of them." The outpouring was complete — it was in full. Since then God has never given more because He gave the complete package on the day of Pentecost. Every person today who so desires *can* be born again and filled with the gift from the Holy Spirit because it is here.

> Verse 4:
> And they [the twelve apostles] were all filled with the Holy Ghost, and began to speak with other tongues, as the Spirit gave them utterance.

They all were filled with *pneuma hagion*, the *gift* from the *Giver*. Not one was missed. Not one received less than any other, nor did any receive more.

There is no article "the" preceding *pneuma hagion* in Acts 2:4 in any of the critical Greek texts. The translators of the King James Version added the article. The Word specifically says that they were all filled with *pneuma hagion*. In Acts 1:4 and 5 and Luke 24:49, we learned that the apostles were told to

86

wait for the power from on high. They obeyed God's Word and were filled with the gift from the Giver, which is inherent spiritual power, *dunamis,* the new birth, "Christ in you." The apostles were all filled with the gift. And once a person has the gift, he can operate it and bring it into manifestation. Verse 4 states this.

Acts 2:4:
... they ... began to speak with other tongues, as the Spirit gave them utterance.

Who began to speak? They, the twelve apostles, began to speak. The subject pronoun "they" is omitted before the second verb, "began," in verse 4 to grammatically emphasize the truth that it was the twelve apostles who began to speak — not the Holy Spirit. The Holy Spirit did not do the speaking for it says that "they ... began to speak ...." The twelve apostles who had just received the gift did the speaking by the power of God which had just been given to them as a gift. And when they began to speak, they spoke "with other tongues ...."

Having received the gift, *pneuma hagion,* they then had the ability to manifest outwardly the inherent power which they had received, and they spoke in tongues a language unknown to their understanding. The reason the apostles could speak in other tongues was that they had received the gift from God; they

87

had not received the gift of speaking in tongues, but the gift of *pneuma hagion,* holy spirit. This truth cannot be overemphasized. It was the apostles themselves who did the speaking, but what they spoke was "as the Spirit [the *pneuma*] gave them utterance." Did the Spirit give to the apostles' minds the words they uttered? No. God being spirit can speak to spirit only.

Pentecost was the first time in history that men had been born again and filled with power from the Holy Spirit, making it possible for God to communicate to their spirits that which their minds did not comprehend. Thus they brought forth the gift into evidence through the manifestation of speaking in tongues. The great miracle of Pentecost was not *that* the apostles spoke in tongues, but *what* they spoke, which was "as the Spirit gave them utterance." What a tremendous and accurate verse of Scripture! It is astounding how Satan could have blinded our eyes to this simple, yet great and magnificent truth so beautifully set forth in this verse.

In four verses the Word of God informs us of the wonderful outpouring of the gift from the Holy Spirit on the day of Pentecost. Acts 1:5 foretells this specific one-time event: "Ye shall be baptized with the Holy Ghost [*pneuma hagion*]." And then Acts 2:1–4 relates the historical moment of that happening. Carefully note that after Pentecost there is no instruction to wait or tarry to receive the gift from the Holy Spirit. Since God gave *pneuma hagion* as a gift, it is here now for anyone to receive at any time.

Verse 5:
And there were dwelling at Jerusalem Jews,* devout men, out of every nation under heaven.

It is very important to note that according to the Word of God, Judeans by religion were the only ones present on the day of Pentecost, and were the only ones who received the gift from the Holy Spirit at that time. The twelve apostles were Galileans. There were many others present in Jerusalem at that time because it was the Jewish Feast of Pentecost, referred to in the Old Testament as the Feast of Weeks or the Feast of First Fruits. Later on we will see the unfolding of the gift from the Holy Spirit to the Gentiles, but not at the time of the historic outpouring on Pentecost.

Verse 6:
Now when this was noised abroad ....

The momentousness of this outpouring was so astounding to those Jews, "devout men," who were present for this Feast of Pentecost, that word of what

*The word "Jew" and its derivatives as used in the KJV should always be understood as meaning "Judean" or "of the Judean religion." The word "Jew" was never in any text until 1775.

had occurred in the Temple spread throughout the city like wildfire.

Verse 6:
... the multitude came together, and were con-founded, because that every man heard them speak in his own language.

The thing that confounded these men was what they heard these twelve apostles speaking in tongues, as it states in verse 4. The tongues in which they were speaking were unknown to the speakers themselves, the twelve apostles, but the tongues were not unknown to the hearers. Each of the "devout men" heard the apostles "speak in his own language." The explanation of this is very simple. The apostles did the speaking in tongues, but what they spoke was not from their minds or human knowledge. This is the miracle of Pentecost that the hearers understood all the apostles were speaking in tongues. What the apostles spoke was from God who is the Holy Spirit. They spoke "as the Spirit gave them utterance." The act of speaking was the apostles' responsibility. What they spoke was God's responsibility.

Verses 7, 8:
And they [the multitude that had come together] were all amazed and marvelled, saying one to another, Behold, are not all these which speak Galileans?

And how hear we every man in our own tongue, wherein we were born?

At what were they amazed and at what did they marvel? They marvelled at hearing their own languages and dialects spoken by these Galilean apostles, whose native tongue was Northern Aramaic.* At that time the other Judeans had very little respect for Galileans but on this occasion their fluency in speaking in tongues was an amazing thing which could not be denied. The apostles speaking in tongues which were strange to themselves but recognizable to the visiting multitude was indeed one of the miracles of Pentecost.

The next 3 verses list the people who were present from the various nations of the world.

> Verses 9—11:
> Parthians, and Medes, and Elamites, and the dwellers in Mesopotamia, and in Judaea, and Cappadocia, in Pontus, and Asia.
>
> Phrygia, and Pamphylia, in Egypt, and in the parts of Libya about Cyrene, and strangers of Rome, Jews and proselytes,
>
> Cretes and Arabians, we do hear them speak in our tongues the wonderful works of God.

*These Galileans knew no other language but their own. Northern Aramaic was different from Southern Aramaic, and at the time of the crucifixion it was by Peter's speech that the little maid was able to identify him as one of Jesus' disciples (Matthew 26:73).

What did they hear them speak? They heard the twelve apostles who were speaking in tongues "speak the wonderful works of God." When we speak in tongues, which is the external evidence in the senses world of the internal presence of the gift from the Holy Spirit, we too are speaking "the wonderful works of God." The Judeans who gave this testimony regarding the Galileans who were speaking in tongues, were not as yet born again of God's Spirit themselves, nor did they have love in their hearts for the Galileans; yet their testimony of what was happening was undeniable — these men were speaking the wonderful works of God.

> Verse 12:
> And they were all amazed [as we were informed in verse 7], and were in doubt, saying one to another, What meaneth this?

Naturally they would be in doubt because they could not understand how Galileans could do this; and when a person does not understand, he cannot help but doubt. Those sincere Judeans questioned in amazement: What is the meaning of this? What is the purpose of it? What is it all about?

> Verses 13,14:
> Others mocking said [those who simply were insincere, mocked and they said], These men are full of new wine.

> But Peter, standing up with the eleven [again the twelve apostles], lifted up his voice, and said unto them, Ye men of Judaea, and all ye that dwell at Jerusalem, be this known unto you, and hearken to my words.

In other words, Peter got up with the eleven and spoke for all twelve of the apostles. He addressed his words to the men of Judea and to all those who were dwelling at Jerusalem at this time of the Jewish Feast of Pentecost. He spoke to them.

Verse 15:
For these are not drunken, as ye suppose, seeing it is *but* the third hour of the day.

Nine o'clock in the morning, which was an hour of prayer, was too early for them to be drunk.*

*The deriding accusation of verse 13 — "These men are full of new wine" — posits the question of whether this "new wine," was of alcoholic content or simply newly-juiced grapes. From all the various texts and translations I have studied I have not been able to acquire sufficient evidence to speak conclusively regarding the matter.

"Wine" in the Bible is used in the sense of being both freshly-made grape juice, and wine with alcoholic content. Usually the context will indicate the usage

In verse 13 "Full of new wine," is one of the problems. Why use the word "new" if it is intoxicating wine? Is "new wine" more intoxicating? Certainly not. Thus it would indicate the "new wine," as being newly-juiced grapes. But verse 15 then presents a problem, for Peter says "... these are not drunken, as ye suppose."

Why would they ever suppose them to be drunken if it was only grape juice they were drinking? "... It is *but* the third hour of the day" complicates matters because they never celebrate with the firstfruits of

Verse 16:

But this is that which was spoken by the prophet Joel;

The question naturally arises as to what is "this" and what is "that." A literal and accurate translation according to context usage would be, "But this is like that which was spoken by the prophet Joel." The word "but" sets what follows in contrast. The word "this" is emphatic, indicating that the quotation from Joel 2:28—32 is used to prove that the charge of drunkenness would not stand concerning the present receiving of the *pneuma hagion* any more so than a charge of drunkenness would stand against

new grape juice early in the day but always after the twelfth hour (6 P.M.)

Jeremiah 25:10 has a descriptive presentation that can be understood only when we understand Eastern customs and practices. "Moreover I will take from them the voice of mirth, and the voice of gladness, the voice of of the bridegroom, and the voice of the bride, the sound of the millstones, and the light of the candle."

The Eastern people celebrate by giving thanks, singing, clapping their hands and beating drums at the firstfruits of corn and rice. They meet on the threshing floor at the close of the day, cook some firstfruits of corn or rice, eat it and rejoice. This is the "voice of mirth."

The "voice of gladness' is the firstfruits of the grape harvest, when they meet after the evening meal, squeeze the juice from some first-fruits grapes, called wine, and drink it, and out of their hearts they rejoice, singing and praising God loudly.

The "voice of the bridegroom" is: John 14:1—4.

The "voice of the bride" is: Ruth 3:5.

The "sound of the millstone" refers to grinding wheat or corn by turning the upper millstone.

The "light of the candle" refers to that perpetually-lighted lamp which is never allowed to go out, representing the presence of God who is Eternal Light.

94

Joel's prophecy of the future outpouring. The word "afterward" in Joel 2:28, translated "in the last days" in Acts 2:17, indicates that Joel's prophecy is not quoted to prove that this present experience was the fulfillment of it. Rather, it is quoted to show that as the prophesied future scene could not be attributed to drunkenness, so this present scene could not be ascribed to drunkenness either.

Then Peter goes on to give forth a message beginning with verse 17 of Acts 2. I often marvel at this message because Peter had no time to go into his office and prepare his sermon before reading his manuscript to his critics. Then how was it possible for him to come forth on the spur of the moment with such a presentation as we find in verses 17 and following of this second chapter of Acts? The answer is very simple. First of all, he had studied the Word of God before this hour; and secondly, he was now filled with the power, the gift, from the Holy Spirit. Jesus had said that men filled with God's gift need not be concerned about what they would say, for even that very hour it would be given unto them. The message of Peter in their language is almost straight prophecy, not foretelling but forthtelling in this instance.

Remember that Peter's message was specifically

addressed to Jews by religion. In verse 36 Peter is coming to the conclusion of his message.

Acts 2:36:
Therefore let all the house of Israel know assuredly, that God hath made that same Jesus, whom ye have crucified, both Lord and Christ.

Another truth that astounded me was the change in Peter's personality. A few short weeks before this, at the time of the crucifixion of our Lord and Savior Jesus Christ, Peter, who had said to the Lord face to face, "I will never deny you," had denied Him and had also fled when the soldiers came to capture the Lord. After the resurrection, Peter, with the rest of the apostles, was behind locked doors "for fear of the Jews," as John 20:19 tells. Now Peter stands calmly before these same Judeans and accuses them in forceful words, "that same Jesus, whom ye have crucified." He does not say, "whom *we* have crucified" but "whom ye have crucified."

That which changed Peter from a vacillating disciple into an apostle who was absolutely fearless and bold was receiving the gift from the Holy Spirit on the day of Pentecost. The record in Acts 2 is the only thing that stands between the resurrection and

Peter's boldness as we find it recorded in this thirty-sixth verse. The only thing I have ever seen that removes fear, changing a fearful soul into one who is bold and confident, is receiving the gift from the Holy Spirit.

Verse 37:
Now when they [those of the house of Israel, Jews by religion] heard *this,* they were pricked in their heart, and said unto Peter and to the rest of the apostles, Men *and* brethren, what shall we do?

When the Judeans had heard the miracle of the Galileans' speaking in tongues "the wonderful works of God," they had been amazed and questioned, "What meaneth this?" Now under the powerful preaching of Peter they were convicted of their guilt of having crucified Jesus and cried out, "What shall we do?"

Verse 38:
Then Peter said unto them, Repent, and be baptized every one of you in the name of Jesus Christ for the remission of sins ....

Peter instructed them to repent. When we repent, we receive remission of sins; not forgiveness, but remission. All the sins which are upon the individual who repents are remitted, are wiped out at the time of salvation.*

Verse 38:

... and ye shall receive [*lambanō*, receive into manifestation] the gift of [from] the Holy Ghost [*pneuma hagion*].

Peter's specific statement, "and ye shall receive" in this grammatical usage means, "and you shall [absolutely] receive [*lambanō*, manifest, show forth in evidence] the gift of [from] the Holy Spirit [*pneuma hagion*]" who is the Giver.† In other words, Peter said that the one who repents receives remission of sins, and he then should absolutely manifest,

---

*"To repent" is not to confess your sins, but to confess the Savior from sin, the Lord Jesus Christ. The confession of sins is works; therefore, repentance cannot be synonymous with the confession of sins for Ephesians 2:8 and 9 tell us that salvation is of grace, not of works. "To repent" is to confess with your mouth the Lord Jesus and to believe within the innermost part of your being that God raised Jesus Christ from the dead. For with the innermost part of your being, you believe unto righteousness and with your mouth confession is made unto salvation (Romans 10:9,10). Thus, repentance is for the unsaved sinner; confession of sins is for the saved sinner (I John 1:9).

A natural man is dead in trespasses and sins without God and without hope in this world. When he confesses with his mouth the Lord Jesus, believing that God raised Him from the dead, he is baptized in the name of Jesus Christ. This baptism is eternal life, Christ in you, the hope of glory, a one-time occurrence. Thus, the new birth is to be baptized in the name of Jesus Christ which includes everything that name represents.

†"I shall" or "we shall" is the simple future tense. "I will" or "we will" denotes absoluteness in the future tense. "You will" is the simple future tense. "You shall" denotes absoluteness in the future tense. "He, she, it will" or "they will" is the simple future tense. "He, she, it shall" or "they shall" denotes absoluteness in the future tense.

lambanō, by speaking in tongues. This was what the apostles manifested on the day of Pentecost when they received the gift, holy spirit, from the Giver, Holy Spirit.

What was the evidence in the external senses world that the gift from the Holy Spirit had been received at Pentecost? The evidence was speaking in tongues. On this occasion when Peter was preaching, the speaking in tongues was all Peter knew about as the evidence that follows when a man is born again and receives remission of his sins; then a believer should manifest, *lambanō*, the gift by speaking in tongues.

Note carefully that on the day of Pentecost, at the outpouring of the gift from the Holy Spirit, Peter delivered a sermon to the assembled people. He had no time to prepare a manuscript. He simply spoke forth the wonderful Word of God as it was given to him, which so stirred his hearers that they cried out, "What shall we do?" Peter did not reply, "Be baptized with the Holy Ghost." He knew by divine revelation that the baptism of or from the Holy Spirit had been given to him and the other apostles, and from Pentecost on there would not be a question of God's gift being given again, but only of man's receiving what had already been given. Therefore, Peter instructed them to repent, be baptized in the name of Jesus Christ for the remission of their sins, "and ye shall receive [*lambanō*] the gift of [from] the Holy Ghost [*pneuma hagion*]." There is no longer a baptism of the holy spirit, it is now a receiving of what God made available on the day of Pentecost. Here is a tremendous truth which must be recognized according to the accuracy of the Word of God. Frequently today we hear people still speaking of being "baptized with the Holy Ghost." We should know, if we are reading the Scriptures accurately, that the phrase "baptized with the Holy Ghost" is never used in The Word after the day of Pentecost.* Over nineteen hundred years of having the revealed Word of God and some still are not reading it accurately! Some people are influenced more by tradition than by the teaching of the Scriptures.

Acts 2:39:
For the promise is unto you [Israel], and to your children [the children of Israel], and to all that are afar off, *even* as many as the Lord our God shall call.

Isn't that wonderful! Peter here explains that the promise as given in verse 38 is first to Israel and to the children of Israel, then to all who will believe. "To all who are afar off, *even* as many as the Lord shall call." Has God called you? If you have repented and received remission of sins, if you are a Christian,

*Acts 11:16 uses these words, but as a quote in recalling the occurrence recorded in Acts 2.

born again of His Spirit, God has called you. The promise is that you shall receive, *lambanō,* the gift from the Holy Spirit if you hear His voice and accept Him. As a result, therefore, you shall be given power to manifest, *lambanō,* the internal reality of the presence of the gift by speaking in tongues the "wonderful works of God."

CHAPTER SEVEN

A Study of Acts 8

Acts 8 is the second record in the book of Acts of anyone's receiving the gift from the Holy Spirit. The events recorded in the eighth chapter of Acts took place several years after the historic outpouring recorded in Acts 2. Remember that only Judeans by religion received the gift at that time, and the proof in the senses world that they had received was that they spoke in tongues.

No new religious group is viciously attacked at its beginning; but as the adherents increase, as the information which they represent becomes disseminated among others, then gradually persecution sets in. In Acts 8 we read about the persecution which had started in Jerusalem because of the growth of the Christian community. According to chapter 7,

Stephen had been stoned.

Acts 8:1, 3 and 4:
And Saul was consenting unto his death. And at that time there was a great persecution against the church which was at Jerusalem; and they [the believers — the Christians] were all scattered abroad throughout the regions of Judaea and Samaria, except the apostles.

As for Saul, he made havock of the church, entering into every house, and haling men and women committed *them* to prison.

Therefore they that were scattered abroad went every where preaching the word.

Note very carefully that even in the midst of the persecution, wherever these Christian leaders went, they did not water-down nor soft-pedal the great accuracy of the Word of God. They did one thing; namely, they preached The Word.

Verse 5:
Then Philip went down to the city of Samaria, and preached Christ unto them.

Philip was one of the seven chosen by the disciples in the early Church according to the record in Acts 6.

104

They chose him to serve tables. God chose him to serve the Bread of Life.

Philip preached the Word of God unto the Samaritans. The Samaritans were disliked by the Judeans, but the ministry was moving out from the center of Judaism in Jerusalem to Samaria.

Verse 6:
And the people with one accord [unity of purpose] gave heed unto those things which Philip spake, hearing and seeing the miracles which he did.

The only reason these Samaritans listened to Philip and what he spoke regarding the Word of God and the Lord Jesus Christ was that they heard and saw the miracles which he, Philip, did. *Philip did the miracles.* Note this truth carefully. He did them by the power of God within him. It does not say God did the miracles. This truth must be recognized and understood because so many people are waiting for God to act when God has already acted. God is waiting for man to receive what He has made available and then act for Him by the power of God.

Verse 7:
For unclean spirits, crying with loud voice, came out of many that were possessed *with them*: and

many taken with palsies, and that were lame, were healed.

Philip spoke the Word of God to the Samaritans and when they heard this Word of God they believed because of the unclean spirits which were cast out by Philip. When the Samaritans saw this happen by the power of God living within Philip, they reacted with excitement.

Verse 8:
And there was great joy in that city.

The Samaritans were rejoicing because people were being saved and healed by the power of God manifested by Philip who was a believer filled with the power or gift from the Holy Spirit.

Verse 9:
But there was a certain man, called Simon, which beforetime in the same city used sorcery, and bewitched the people of Samaria, giving out that himself was some great one.

Simon, before the coming of Philip, used sorcery (witchcraft, spiritualism, black arts, ESP, operation of devil spirits), and by the operation of devil spirits he had for many years deceived and controlled the people of Samaria.

Verses 10,11:
To whom they all gave heed, from the least to the greatest, saying, This man [Simon] is the great power of God.

And to him they had regard, because that of long time he had bewitched them with sorceries.

These people had been hoodwinked and were under the control of Simon the sorcerer because they believed his operation of devil spirits was evidence of "the great power of God."

Verse 12:
But when they [the Samaritans] believed Philip preaching the things concerning the kingdom of God, and the name of Jesus Christ, they were baptized, both men and women.

When the Samaritans believed the Word of God which Philip preached, they repented and were saved. People may be under the spell of the preaching and teaching of men who use, or who are used by, devil spirits. But when the truth of the power of the Word of God is made known by a man filled with the holy spirit, manifesting signs, miracles, and wonders and proving The Word, some people will believe and be saved. This is what happened in Samaria.

107

Verse 13:

Then Simon himself believed also ....

What happened to Simon? He was converted. He believed The Word that Philip preached, which is Christ, and when Simon believed on the Lord Jesus Christ, he received salvation. Simon, who had been operating devil spirits and bewitching the people of Samaria for so many years, was saved under the ministry of Philip. This is a tremendous example of the power of the Word of God rightly divided and preached by a man filled with the holy spirit.

Verse 13:

Then Simon himself believed also: and when he was baptized, he continued with Philip, and wondered, beholding the miracles and signs which were done.

What did Simon wonder about? He wondered how Philip could do these signs and miracles. Simon knew from his experience among the people of Samaria that he himself had done tremendous feats, and he was under no illusions as to the source of his authority and power which came from devil spirits working through sorcery and the black arts. But as Simon continued to observe Philip's miracles and signs, he remained puzzled as to Philip's source of power.

This certainly emphasizes the error of the teaching that if a man is born again he automatically has a renewed mind and walks in great truth. Simon was born again, but his mind was still in error regarding the working of the gift of holy spirit.

The following verse in Acts 8 tells us that Peter and John then made a visit to Samaria.

Verse 14:
Now when the apostles which were at Jerusalem heard that Samaria had received the word of God, they sent unto them Peter and John.

What triggered Peter and John's going to Samaria? The reason that the apostles Peter and John, the heads of the Church, came from Jerusalem to Samaria was that there was an unprecedented occurrence in the Church in Samaria — those who had been born again were not speaking in tongues. This was the first time in the history of the Christian Church that the manifestation of speaking in tongues was not in evidence immediately following the new birth. The two great leaders among the apostles went down to investigate this strange happening.

The people in Samaria who had heard the Word of God and believed what Philip preached, had received spiritually, *dechomai.* They had spiritually received the new birth, the power, the gift from the Holy

109

Spirit; but they had not manifested anything in the senses world. Therefore, Peter and John came down from Jerusalem.

Verse 15:
Who, when they were come down, prayed for them, that they might receive [*lambanō*] the Holy Ghost [*pneuma hagion*]:

They had spiritually received, *dechomai*, but they had not received into manifestation, *lambanō*. When Peter and John came down from Jerusalem, they prayed for the new believers that they might *lambanō*, manifest forth, the holy spirit, which they had received as a gift from the Giver at the time they were saved.

Verse 16:
(For as yet he was fallen upon none of them [the holy spirit had not been manifested]: only they were baptized in the name of the Lord Jesus.)

In the Aramaic there is no neuter gender. Therefore, the translation of the third person singular would be "he." However, many times in translation "he" should be, and is, translated "it" as in Romans 8:16.* "It was fallen upon none of them." The word

*Romans 8:16: "The Spirit itself beareth witness with our spirit, that we are the children of God."

110

"fallen" is *epipiptō*, and the word "upon" is *epi.* "Fallen upon" is *epipiptō epi. Piptō* means "to fall." *Epipiptō* therefore means "to fall from upon a higher plane." *Epi*, "upon," by itself is used with the dative case, indicating actual super-position (at rest upon) — the result of the *epipiptō*, falling from a higher plane. Therefore the phrase "fallen upon none of them" literally means "fallen from upon a higher plane to a position at rest on a lower plane, i.e. "from upon" (*epipiptō*) the spiritual plane to the "at rest upon" (*epi*) in manifestation in the natural realm.

Verse 17:
Then laid they *their* hands on them, and they received [*lambanō*] the Holy Ghost [*pneuma hagion*].

The apostles, Peter and John, laid their hands upon the believers who had before received the Lord Jesus Christ, *dechomai*, but had not received, *lambanō*, manifested, the gift in the senses world.

The "laying on of hands" is used in the Word of God to identify the person ministering with the one being ministered to. Furthermore, when hands are laid on, it is for revelation manifestations (namely, the word of knowledge, the word of wisdom and the discerning of spirits   three of the nine manifestations of the spirit) to be put into operation.

111

By the revelation manifestations, Peter and John received the information as to why the people of Samaria had spiritually received the new birth, the power from the Holy Spirit, but had not manifested it in the senses world. Whatever it was that had been blocking the Christians of Samaria from manifesting *pneuma hagion*, Peter and John, having laid their hands on them, and knowing by revelation what the hindering obstacle was, cast it out in the name of Jesus Christ, and then the Samaritan Christians received, *lambanō*, manifested, *pneuma hagion*.

From just a cursory reading of Acts 8 and without the understanding of the operation of the nine manifestations of the spirit, it would be difficult to rightly divide it. Reading verses nine through eleven, we know that devil spirits had so infiltrated the Samaritans that, of the three revelation manifestations of the holy spirit, discerning of spirits must have been very much in operation.

These Samaritans had been bewitched a long time by Simon. There is a truth here that all Christians need to recognize. I John 4:4 straightforwardly states, "... greater is he that is in you, than he that is in the world." All hell cannot stop a man from being born again and receiving the power or gift from the Holy Spirit when he believes according to Romans 10:9. All the devil spirits in the world are not strong

112

enough to withstand the power from the Holy Spirit. Satan could not stop the Samaritans from being saved, nor can Satan stop anyone from being saved because salvation is a gift and anyone who desires to receive *can* receive that gift of salvation and be filled with the power from the Holy Spirit when he believes.

It is not stated in Acts 8 that when the Samaritans received *pneuma hagion* they spoke in tongues. But I would like for you to carefully note verse 18.

Acts 8:18:
And when Simon saw that through laying on of the apostles' hands the Holy Ghost [the *pneuma*, the *hagion*] was given, he offered them money.

Let me ask you, "What did Simon see?" One cannot see spirit. One cannot see the new birth, for Christ in you, the new birth, is spirit. Therefore, what did Simon see when these apostles, Peter and John, laid hands on the believers who had accepted the Lord Jesus Christ? What Simon saw had to be in the senses world, something visible, something that was manifested. Therefore, Simon saw a manifestation of the spirit which must have been speaking in tongues, because in every other instance where the manifestation of the holy spirit is mentioned, it is always

113

speaking in tongues.

Verse 19:
Saying, Give me also this power, that on whomsoever I lay hands, he may receive [*lambanō*] the Holy Ghost [*pneuma hagion*].

By the laying on of hands nothing is automatically communicated. You cannot give anyone something unless that person wants it and you cannot give anything if you do not have it. Peter said to the lame man at the Temple gate, as recorded in Acts 3:6, "Such as I have give I thee: In the name of Jesus Christ of Nazareth rise up and walk." The laying on of hands by revelation is a means of identifying the person ministering with the one who is in need, and then the revelation manifestations are in operation.

Simon could not have seen spirit, but he saw that things happened when the apostles laid their hands on the Samaritan believers. Then he said to Peter and John, "Give me also this power [give to me this ministry of an apostle]." And "he offered them money." He was willing to pay money for the ministry of an apostle thinking that on whomsoever he might lay his hands, that person would manifest, *lambanō, pneuma hagion.* But a ministry cannot be bought; a ministry is not earned; a ministry in the

114

body of the Church is a gift of God.*

Acts 8:20:
But Peter said unto him, Thy money perish with
thee, because thou hast thought that the gift of
God may be purchased with money.

Peter said, "Thy money perish with thee." The
Greek word for "perish" means "to rot." When a
person is born again of God's Spirit, having received
eternal life, and Simon had been born again as told in
verse 13, he can no longer perish spiritually. "Thy
money perish with thee" does not mean that Peter said
to Simon that he was to lose his eternal life. He was explaining to Simon that just as the body perishes, disin-
tegrates, rots, so the money that Simon had offered for
this ministry, "the gift of God," would perish with
him — with his body. Notice the word "thought."
After a person is born again of God's Spirit, *he* must
renew his mind according to The Word, and this
changing of the mind is usually a slow process. This
explains why Simon "wondered" when he saw the
miracles and signs performed by Philip. His mind had
not been renewed and he thought it might be possible
to buy such a ministry. Simon, though born again,
had not put on the mind of Christ because he thought

*Ephesians 4:8,11: "Wherefore he saith, When he ascended up on high,
he led captivity captive, and gave gifts unto men. And he gave some,
apostles; and some, prophets; and some, evangelists; and some, pastors
and teachers."

115

"that the gift of God [Here, the ministry of an apostle is called the gift of God.]" could be purchased with money.

Peter continues to upbraid Simon in verse 21.

Acts 8:21:
Thou hast neither part nor lot in this matter: for thy heart is not right in the sight of God.

The word "matter" should be the word "ministry." The word "heart" indicates the seat of the personal life. Simon had been born again of God's Spirit, but his personal life was wrong. His thoughts were wrong; he was out of fellowship with God.

Verse 22:
Repent therefore of this thy wickedness ....

The word "repent" must be translated "forsake." When one repents he receives remission of sins.* He must then forsake his wickedness. According to Acts 8:13, Simon himself believed and repented when he was converted. A person can only repent once. After salvation, it is still possible to sin if we have not put on the mind of Christ. If our thoughts are not His

*Acts 2:38: "Then Peter said unto them, Repent, and be baptized every one of you in the name of Jesus Christ for the remission of sins, and ye shall receive the gift of the Holy Ghost."

thoughts, our minds are not His mind. Simon, therefore, is instructed by Peter that he is to forsake this wickedness of trying to buy the ministry of an apostle.

Verse 22:
Repent therefore of this thy wickedness and pray God, if perhaps [the word "perhaps" in the critical Greek text reads "that"] the thought of thine heart may be forgiven thee.

Verse 22 should literally be translated, "Forsake therefore of this thy wickedness and pray God that the thoughts of your mind may be forgiven thee." It does not say that they may be repented of, but may be forgiven. Once we are born again of God's Spirit and we sin, we must confess our sin which is broken fellowship with God, and He is according to I John 1:9, "faithful and just to forgive us *our* sins, and to cleanse us from all unrighteousness."

Acts 8:23-25:
For I perceive that thou art in the gall of bitterness, and *in* the bond of iniquity. [This Peter knew by revelation, word of knowledge.]

Then answered Simon, and said, Pray ye to the Lord for me, that none of these things which ye have spoken come upon me.

And they, when they had testified and preached the word of the Lord, returned to Jerusalem, and preached the gospel in many villages of the Samaritans.

Peter and John had accomplished their mission in Samaria. They had instructed the Samaritans as to the power they had received (*dechomai*) and the Samaritans then manifested (*lambanō*) the evidences of the gift from the Holy Spirit.

CHAPTER EIGHT

A Study of Acts 9

The third reference in the book of Acts regarding anyone's receiving the gift from the Holy Spirit is found in the ninth chapter of Acts. Saul, after persecuting the Church in the Jerusalem community, headed for Damascus. On the road to Damascus, he who had persecuted and injured the Church so viciously was converted and had to be led by the hand into the city of Damascus. According to Acts 9:9, "he was three days without sight, and neither did eat nor drink." Verse 10 begins the third great teaching which is a continued unfolding of all the Bible teaches regarding the receiving of the gift from the Holy Spirit.

In this record we have not a group, but a single individual. "Saul" was his Hebrew name; his Greek name was "Paul."

From the record in Acts 8 certain teachers have constantly implied that only heads of the Church like Peter and John could minister the holy spirit. This misconception has been carried down through the centuries through various sects. These teachers cite Philip's saying that he was only a disciple and not one of the heads of the Church; therefore, he could not minister the holy spirit. But that cannot be true, because of what we see in Acts 9.

Acts 9:10:
And there was a certain disciple at Damascus, named Ananias; and to him said the Lord in a vision, Ananias. And he said, Behold, I *am here*, Lord.

Ananias was not an apostle, a Peter or a John. He was just a "certain disciple." In Acts 9:10 and following we see that this certain disciple named Ananias ministered to one who was to be the greatest of all the apostles, the Apostle Paul.

Verses 11–20:
And the Lord *said* unto him [Ananias], Arise, and go into the street which is called Straight, and inquire in the house of Judas for *one* called Saul, of Tarsus: for, behold, he prayeth,

And hath seen in a vision a man named Ananias

coming in, and putting *his* hand on him, that he might receive his sight.

Then Ananias answered, Lord, I have heard by many of this man, how much evil he hath done to thy saints at Jerusalem:

And here he hath authority from the chief priests to bind all that call on thy name.

But the Lord said unto him, Go thy way: for he is a chosen vessel unto me, to bear my name before the Gentiles, and kings, and the children of Israel:

For I will shew him how great things he must suffer for my name's sake.

And Ananias went his way, and entered into the house; and putting his hands on him said, Brother Saul, the Lord, *even* Jesus, that appeared unto thee in the way as thou camest, hath sent me, that thou mightest receive thy sight, and be filled with the Holy Ghost [*pneuma hagion*].

And immediately there fell from his eyes as it had been scales: and he received sight forthwith, and arose, and was baptized.

121

And when he had received meat, he was strengthened. Then was Saul certain days with the disciples which were at Damascus.

And straightway he preached Christ in the synagogues, that he is the Son of God.

Ananias, just a disciple, was informed by the Lord that he was to arise and go into the street called Straight. (By the way, that is the only manner whereby he could possibly get into that street; because the street called Straight runs east and west all the way through the city of Damascus, and the house of Ananias is located on a street which dead-ends directly into the street called Straight. The marvelous accuracy of the Word of God is astounding.) And the Lord told Ananias that he would find Paul in the house of Judas, and Paul would be praying. What a tremendous amount of information!

The Lord told Ananias exactly what to do and where he would find Paul, and he even told him what Paul would be doing. I venture to say that when Ananias arrived in the house of Judas, Paul was not sitting around holding a conversation with people; he was not singing nor shouting, but he was doing what the Word of God said: he was praying.

I want you to note also that Ananias did not like the job which the Lord was giving him. In other words, Ananias did not want to do the Word of God. This is why Ananias spoke back to the Lord and this is the right thing to do. If you and I do not like the Word of God as God has given it, we ought to talk to God about it. We ought not to criticize the people who believe. Go back to the source. This is exactly what Ananias did; he talked to the Lord. In effect he said, "Lord, I have heard by many of the evil this man has done, and here in Damascus he has the authority from the chief priests to bind all the people who are Christians, who call on Thy name. So why are you now asking me, simple old Ananias, to do something which I just do not want to do?" But the Lord gave Ananias more information. He said, "Go thy way for he [Paul] is a chosen vessel unto me."

Verse 17:
And Ananias went his way ....

Ananias literally acted upon the revealed Word of God. He went from his house into the street called Straight and he entered into the house of Judas. There he found Paul praying. Then Ananias went in and put his hands on him. The reason he put his hands on Paul was for the revelation manifestations to go into operation, namely, word of knowledge, word of wisdom and discerning of spirits. In this way

Ananias could carry out the job of delivering Paul who was blind, and who had not as yet received into manifestation the gift from the Holy Spirit. He put his hands on him and said — note very carefully — "Brother Saul."

In the East no one refers to a person as a brother unless he means it. The reason Ananias could refer to Paul as a brother is because the Lord had told Ananias that Paul was converted on the road to Damascus, and when a man is converted, born again of God's Spirit, having the same spirit that every born-again son of God has, he becomes a brother to all other Christians. Not everyone in the world is my brother, but those who are born again by God's Spirit are my brothers.

> Acts 9:17:
> And Ananias went his way, and entered into the house; and putting his hands on him said, Brother Saul, the Lord, *even* Jesus, that appeared unto thee in the way as thou camest, hath sent me, that thou mightest receive thy sight, and be filled with the Holy Ghost.

Ananias told Paul that God was responsible for his coming to minister sight and to minister *pneuma hagion*, the holy spirit, to him.

124

Verse 18:

And immediately there fell from his eyes as it had been scales: and he received sight ....

How does one gain sight when men of God who are filled with the holy spirit minister? The person being ministered to must receive it, he has to take it, he must believe. In this verse it does not say that Paul received the gift from the Holy Spirit, but that the Lord told Ananias to minister sight and that Paul might "be filled with *pneuma hagion*," which is to be filled with the gift in manifestation. It does not say Paul spoke in tongues, but he must have, because the task that Ananias set out to do was not only to minister healing, but also to minister to him the gift from the Holy Spirit into manifestation. I Corinthians 14:18 says, "I [Paul] thank my God, I speak with tongues more than ye all." So the Apostle Paul must have spoken in tongues.

In this third record note carefully that healing and the gift from the Holy Spirit were ministered by a simple disciple, not an apostle, but just a believer born again of God's Spirit. Ananias ministered the holy spirit and healing into manifestation to Paul who immediately went out and witnessed that "Christ ... is the Son of God."

In the three records we have studied thus far, we have seen that in Acts 2, on the day of Pentecost

125

when the twelve received the gift, "they spoke in tongues." In Acts 8, in Samaria, Simon saw something. What could he see but the manifestation in the senses world? In Acts 9 Paul was filled with the holy spirit. It does not specifically say that he spoke in tongues but in I Corinthians 14:18, it does say that he spoke in tongues frequently. Speaking in tongues immediately upon one's salvation clearly is a standard of behavior from the Word of God.

CHAPTER NINE

A Study of Acts 10

Acts 10 is the fourth record in the Word of God regarding anyone's receiving the holy spirit. In this record we see for the first time in the history of the Christian Church that Gentiles received the gift from the Holy Spirit without being proselytes of Judaism. As I indicated earlier, on the day of Pentecost only men of Judaism received; then one individual — the Apostle Paul received. Now we are to consider the first record telling that Gentiles received. This is a tremendously important precedent because never before in the history of the Church had Gentiles as a group ever received without first becoming proselytes to Judaism.

Gentiles had always been looked upon by the Judeans as "dogs," having no part whatsoever in the things of the Lord. In the eyes of Judaism, Samaritans were bad enough, but Gentiles were at the bottom of the barrel. And no decent, ordinary, God-fearing Judean would have anything to do with a Gentile. We are going to see a great innovation take place in the early Church, and we want to note the truths of this chapter carefully.

> Acts 10:1,2:
> There was a certain man in Caesarea called Cornelius, a centurion [leader of a hundred men] of the band called the Italian *band*,
>
> *A* devout *man*, and one that feared God with all his house, which gave much alms to the people, and prayed to God alway.

Cornelius was a religious, devout man, but he was not yet born again of God's Spirit, which indicates that one can be a devout man without being born again.

> Verses 3—6:
> He saw in a vision evidently about the ninth hour of the day [three o'clock in the afternoon in our reckoning] an angel of God coming in to him, and saying unto him, Cornelius.
>
> And when he [Cornelius] looked on him [angel], he was afraid, and said, What is it, Lord? And he said unto him, Thy prayers and

128

thine alms are come up for a memorial before
God.

And now send men to Joppa, and call for *one*
Simon, whose surname is Peter:

He lodgeth with one Simon a tanner, whose
house is by the sea side: he shall tell thee what
thou oughtest to do.

Simon Peter was in the city of Joppa, but really
not in the city proper because he was lodging with a
tanner. A person in the tanning business, because of
the odors involved, was never allowed to live within
the city limits. God told Cornelius by a vision of an
angel that he was to send men to Joppa for Simon
Peter, and Simon Peter would tell him what he should
do.

Verse 7:
And when the angel which spake unto Cornelius
was departed, he called two of his household
servants, and a devout soldier of them that
waited on him continually.

In other words, Cornelius called three men, two of
his household servants and one of the head soldiers
who was under him.

Verse 8:
And when he had declared all *these* things unto
them, he sent them to Joppa.

God had told Cornelius that they were to call for
Simon Peter who was living with Simon the tanner.

Verse 9:
On the morrow [the next day], as they went on
their journey, and drew nigh unto the city, Peter
went up upon the housetop to pray about the
sixth hour.

As these three men who were sent by Cornelius
arrived on the outskirts of the city of Joppa, Peter was
up on the housetop praying, and the time was twelve
o'clock as we reckon time.

Verses 10—16:
And he [Peter] became very hungry, and would
have eaten: but while they made ready [the
food], he fell into a trance [dormant state of
mental awareness],

And saw heaven opened, and a certain vessel
descending unto him, as it had been a great sheet
knit at the four corners, and let down to the
earth [It wasn't a great sheet. It was *like* a great
sheet]:

130

Wherein were all manner of fourfooted beasts of the earth, and wild beasts, and creeping things, and fowls of the air.

And there came a voice to him, Rise, Peter; kill, and eat.

But Peter said, Not so, Lord; for I have never eaten any thing that is common [defiled] or unclean.

And the voice *spake* unto him again the second time, What God hath cleansed, *that* call not thou common.

This was done thrice: and the vessel was received up again into heaven.

How wonderfully accurate is the Word of God, and how perfectly God sets all things in order at the proper time preparing men to carry out His will. Peter was a Judean by religion. He had been born again of God's Spirit on the day of Pentecost and filled with the power from the Holy Spirit, but Peter was still "zealous of the law." So this phenomenon of a vessel descending as a sheet from heaven down to the earth, being filled with all kinds of animals and beasts that no one in Judaism would ever think of eating, and a voice saying, "Rise, Peter; kill, and eat," was a shock and a challenge.

Peter said, "Not so, Lord; for I have never eaten any thing that is common or unclean." But the voice instructed Peter that what had been cleansed by God, Peter had no right to call defiled or unclean. God was beginning to prepare Peter to minister to a Gentile and his household.

Verses 17,18:
Now while Peter doubted in himself what this vision [picture] which he had seen should mean, behold, the men which were sent from Cornelius [the two servants and the soldier] had made inquiry for Simon's house, and stood before the gate,

And called, and asked whether Simon, which was surnamed Peter, were lodged there.

At the very moment Peter was considering the meaning of the vision, the men arrived from the house of Cornelius, "and called." (In the East you do not knock on the door; you stand in front of the gate and call by name the man you are seeking.)

Verse 19:
While Peter thought on the vision [a phenomenon in this instance], the Spirit said unto him, Behold, three men seek thee.

The Spirit revealed further to Peter what was happening. God speaks to men by the three revelation manifestations: word of knowledge, word of wisdom and discerning of spirits.

Verse 20:
Arise therefore, and get thee down, and go with them, doubting nothing: for I have sent them.

The instructions to Peter were very explicit. First of all God had shown to him in a vision what was clean and unclean. Secondly, God specifically spoke to Peter by way of the spirit.

Verse 21:
Then Peter went down to the men which were sent unto him from Cornelius; and said, Behold, I am he whom ye seek: what *is* the cause wherefore ye are come?

The revelation which God gives is beyond that which we can know through our five senses. God did not, by way of the spirit, tell Peter the purpose or the reason for the coming of the men from Cornelius. He simply showed Peter a vision, and by the Spirit told Peter to go down to them and doubt nothing because God had sent them. When Peter came down to meet the three men, he asked them, "What *is* the cause wherefore ye are come?"

Verses 22,23:

And they said, Cornelius the centurion, a just man, and one that feareth God, and of good report among all the nation of the Jews, was warned from God by an holy angel to send for thee into his house, and to hear words of thee.

Then called he [Peter] them [the three men] in, and lodged *them.* And on the morrow Peter went away with them, and certain brethren from Joppa accompanied him.

When the men reported to Peter exactly what God had said by the angel to Cornelius, Peter realized the meaning of his own vision. God had been preparing him to go to Cornelius, a Gentile, and to enter into his house. This is something that no follower of Judaism would voluntarily think of doing. Yet God had instructed him to do so. Peter obediently went with the three men whom Cornelius had sent, and he took with him certain other brethren who were born again of God's Spirit. In this decision we see in operation the manifestation of the spirit called word of wisdom, for Peter knew what the reaction of the apostles in Jerusalem would be when they heard that he had gone into the house of a Gentile. He knew there would be questioning from his religious brethren. Therefore, in order to prepare for this, Peter took witnesses with him so that they could substantiate

134

everything that had happened if he were called to give an account of his unorthodox actions. We see later in Acts 11:12 that Peter actually was called before the brethren in Jerusalem and he reported his activity in the Cornelius household as follows: "And the spirit bade me go with them, nothing doubting. Moreover these six brethren accompanied me, and we entered into the man's [Cornelius'] house."

Verse 24:
And the morrow after they entered into Caesarea. And Cornelius waited for them, and had called together his kinsmen and near friends.

Cornelius was eagerly awaiting Peter's arrival because God had told him that Peter would tell him what he ought to do. Cornelius, being a God-fearing man, wanted to know the will of God; he wanted to carry out God's purpose and plan for his life. Not only was Cornelius waiting for Peter's arrival, but he had called together a group of people, "his kinsmen and near friends." Peter did not have to carry on an advertising campaign when he arrived in Caesarea in order to get a hearing for the Word of God. Cornelius had arranged the meeting so that when Peter arrived all was ready and in order. One thing further we should consider. In the East, the head of a family is responsible for the entire family, and when he speaks, all carry out exactly what he decides. In other words, what the head of a family believes, the rest of the family believes also.

Verse 25:
And as Peter was coming in, Cornelius met him, and fell down at his feet, and worshipped *him*.

It is an Eastern custom that when a man of God comes in, respect is shown to him by falling down at his feet, even endeavoring to reach out and to touch his feet, thereby indicating humility, reverence and respect.

Verse 26:
But Peter took him up, saying, Stand up; I myself also am a man.

Peter, a man born again of God's Spirit, in whom the spirit from God dwelt, realized that he himself was, as far as the human element was concerned, very, very weak and also just a man even as Cornelius was a man.

Verses 27,28:
And as he talked with him, he [Peter] went in, and found many who were come together.

And he said unto them, Ye know how that it is an unlawful thing for a man that is a Jew to keep company, or come unto one of another nation; but God hath shewed me that I should not call any man common or unclean.

God had dealt specifically with Peter and by instructing him in the vision of a great sheet descending from heaven to earth. God had talked to Peter by way of the spirit — word of knowledge and word of wisdom. Peter never would have considered going with the two servants and the soldier that Cornelius had sent to Joppa had God not shown him that he was not to call any man defiled or unclean.

Verse 29:
Therefore come I *unto you* without gainsaying, as soon as I was sent for: I ask therefore for what intent ye have sent for me?

Peter still did not know the full purpose for which Cornelius had sent his soldier and two servants to him. What can be known by the five senses God expects us to know. Revelation (word of knowledge, word of wisdom and discerning of spirits) begins where the information that the five senses can supply ceases. What we can know, God expects us to know. What we can share with one another from the Word of God accurately, God expects us to share. The revelation manifestations of the spirit begin where sense-knowledge ends. So Peter said to Cornelius, "Tell me, for what purpose did you send for me? God has shown me that I am not to call any man defiled or unclean. The Spirit told me that

137

I was to go with the three men who were at the gate, doubting nothing, that God had sent them. Now tell me, why am I here?"

Verses 30–33:
And Cornelius said, Four days ago I was fasting until this hour; and at the ninth hour I prayed in my house, and, behold, a man stood before me in bright clothing,

And said, Cornelius, thy prayer is heard, and thine alms are had in remembrance in the sight of God.

Send therefore to Joppa, and call hither Simon, whose surname is Peter; he is lodged in the house of *one* Simon a tanner by the sea side: who, when he cometh, shall speak unto thee.

Immediately therefore I sent to thee; and thou hast well done that thou art come. Now therefore are we all here present before God, to hear all things that are commanded thee of God.

Note carefully that Cornelius, like Peter, acted literally and immediately upon the revealed Word of God. If you and I expect to receive the results of the Word of God, we must first of all be sure that we have The Word and then we must act upon it immediately and literally; no postponing; we must act on it now!

138

What a tremendous statement Cornelius made when he told Peter that this group of kinsmen and near friends whom he had collected together were present before God. They had assembled themselves together just the same as if God Almighty had stood there. And Cornelius said to Peter. "Now ... we ... to hear all things that are commanded thee of God." Cornelius was not interested in theology, he was not interested in what people said, he was not interested in "apple-polishing," nor in any fanfare. The only thing Cornelius wanted to hear was that which God had commanded Peter to speak. In other words, he wanted to hear only the Word of God — "all things that are commanded thee of God."

> Verse 34:
> Then Peter opened *his* mouth, and said, Of a truth I perceive that God is no respecter of persons.

Through a vision and by revelation of the spirit, God had already informed Peter that nothing in itself is defiled or unclean, and in obedience to the Word of God, Peter had gone to the home of Cornelius who was a Gentile. When Peter began speaking to those gathered together, the first thing Peter said was, "... Of a truth I perceive that God is no respector of persons." This is a meaningful lesson from the Scriptures pointing to those who are filled with prejudice.

139

Until this time the Judeans had always prided themselves on being God's people, that God had given the oracles unto them and not to the Gentiles. But now Peter said by the Word of the Lord that he perceived that God is no respecter of persons. God does not favor persons but He does respect conditions and when those conditions are met, men and women will receive the power from the Holy Spirit. He does not care whether a person is a Judean or a Gentile. He is not concerned about the color of a man's skin. God offers His gift to *all* who will meet His conditions, for "God is no respecter of persons."

Verses 35,36:
But in every nation he that feareth him [has reverence for God], and worketh righteousness, is accepted with him.

The word which *God* sent unto the children of Israel, preaching peace by Jesus Christ: (he is Lord of all:)

"The word which God sent unto the children of Israel" refers to Jesus' coming unto His own. The outpouring on the day of Pentecost was to Judeans only. Yet Peter knew now that God is not only the God of the Judeans, but that He is Lord of all. Every person in every nation who would believe on Him was to be born again and filled with the power from the Holy Spirit.

140

Verses 37,38:

That word, *I say,* ye know, which was published throughout all Judaea, and began from Galilee, after the baptism which John preached;

How God anointed Jesus of Nazareth with the Holy Ghost and with power: who went about doing good, and healing all that were oppressed of the devil; for God was with him.

Here Peter is teaching Cornelius and his household the great truths regarding the Lord Jesus Christ and the power from the Holy Spirit. Peter says in verse 38 that "God anointed Jesus of Nazareth with the Holy Ghost and with power." Literally this could be translated "God anointed Jesus of Nazareth with *pneuma hagion,* holy spirit, which is *dunamis,* inherent power."

In verse 37 Peter alludes to the baptism of Jesus by John the Baptist in the River Jordan, which marked the opening of Jesus' ministry. John was the prophet before Jesus, and John prophesied of Jesus as one far above himself who alone would baptize "with the Holy Ghost, and *with* fire" in Matthew 3:11. John was filled with "the Holy Ghost [*pneuma hagion*], even from his mother's womb," as was prophesied by the angel in Luke 1:15. But Jesus, born of Mary, was *conceived* "of the Holy Ghost," as was told to Joseph

141

by the angel of the Lord, recorded in Matthew 1:20, though Jesus was not filled with *pneuma hagion* from His mother's womb. During His youth Jesus worked and studied the Word of God, and Luke 2:52 says he "increased in wisdom and stature, and in favour with God and man."

Using that inherent power, Jesus went about healing "all that were oppressed of the devil" (verse 38). Sickness came into the world by the sin of man; therefore, because of the origin of sickness and sin, verse 38 does not differentiate between sickness and the activities of Satan. It may be said that all sickness is some form of oppression of the devil, and all healing is deliverance from all manner of diseases by the power of God.

Verse 39:
And we are witnesses of all things which he did both in the land of the Jews, and in Jerusalem; whom they slew and hanged on a tree.

As we read in Acts 1, just before Jesus ascended up into heaven, having gathered the apostles about Him, He told them that they were to wait for the promise from the Father. After they received the promise, they were to be witnesses to the great truth of the power from the Holy Spirit. Peter says we are witnesses of all these things regarding the Lord Jesus whom the Judeans at Jerusalem crucified on a tree.

142

A Study of Acts 10

Verse 40:

Him [this one whom the Jews in Jerusalem hanged on a tree] God raised up the third day ....*

This agrees exactly with Jesus' own words concerning Himself in Matthew 12:40, "... as Jonas was three days and three nights in the whale's belly; so shall the Son of man be three days and three nights in the heart of the earth." I Corinthians 15:4 states "... that he rose again the third day ...." Jesus Christ was dead three days and three nights, and yet God raised Him on the third day and showed Him openly — "openly" meaning that the people saw Him, that there was nothing hidden. He was manifested in the senses world after His resurrection.

Verses 41—43:

Not to all the people [He was not shown openly to all the people.], but unto witnesses chosen before of God, *even* to us, who did eat and drink with him after he rose from the dead.

And he commanded us to preach unto the people, and to testify that it is he which was ordained of God *to be* the Judge of quick [living] and dead.

*Victor Paul Wierwille, *The Word's Way* — *Vol. III, Studies in Abundant Living* (American Christian Press, New Knoxville, Ohio, 1971), chapter 12, "The Day Jesus Christ Died."

To him give all the prophets witness, that through his name whosoever believeth in him shall receive remission of sins.

Peter is instructing the household of Cornelius who had not yet been born again. "Remission of sins" applies only to the unsaved. To be born again one must believe on the Lord Jesus and that God raised Him from the dead. When and at the time a man believes, he receives remission of all sins he has committed in life up to that moment. They are all wiped out at the moment of believing and accepting Jesus as Lord.

Now we come to the concluding section of this fourth great teaching in the book of Acts regarding the new birth, receiving the gift from the Holy Spirit.

Verse 44:
While Peter yet spake these words, the Holy Ghost [the *pneuma*, the *hagion*] fell on all them which heard the word.

While Peter was yet preaching, while he was teaching the Word of God to Cornelius and those assembled in his house, they believed; and without anyone's laying hands on them, *pneuma hagion*, "the promise of the Father," which is to be "baptized with the Holy Ghost," fell upon all of them and they were "endued with power from on high."

Here the word "heard" is not the Greek word meaning to hear only with the physical ears, but to hear to the end of believing by acting on it. This is one time that a man of God who was speaking the Word of God never got to say "Amen." Peter never got to finish his sermon.

Verses 45,46:
And they of the circumcision which believed were astonished, as many as came with Peter, because that on the Gentiles also was poured out the gift of the Holy Ghost [*pneuma hagion*].

For they [Peter and the six brethren who accompanied him] heard them speak with tongues, and magnify God ....

We are told in Acts 10:23 that certain of the brethren of Joppa had accompanied Peter on this journey. These believers who were "of the circumcision" were astonished that the gift fell on the Gentiles for they heard them speak in tongues.

At the outpouring in Jerusalem, those of the circumcision had received the gift from the Holy Spirit. However, that had not been so dramatically surprising as this receiving of the gift, for the circumcision had been taught that Israel could receive things from God because they were God's chosen people. But for

145

Gentiles to receive without becoming proselytes of Judaism was almost unbelievable. These six brethren, the believers who had accompanied Peter, were astonished "because that on the Gentiles also was poured out the gift ...." The word "also" tells us that the Gentiles had received the same gift as those of the circumcision had received years before in Jerusalem. The Word does not say they received the Giver, but the gift from the Giver, the same as in Acts 2:38.

Something happened that day at the house of Cornelius to convince Peter and those who accompanied him that the Gentiles also had received the gift. This something had to be indisputable. It had to be something in the senses world that was so absolute that nobody, not even one "of the circumcision," could deny the truth thereof. Those Gentiles could have been immersed in water time and time again, yet that would never have convinced the Judean believers that the Gentiles actually had been born again of God's Spirit and had received the gift from the Holy Spirit. What could it possibly have been that convinced those present that the Gentiles also had received the gift of *pneuma hagion*? What was the external evidence of the internal reality of the presence of the holy spirit?

The evidence in the senses world that convinced Peter and the six brethren, beyond a shadow of a doubt, was the fact that they heard the Gentiles

146

speak with tongues. Peter and those with him had spoken in tongues and did speak in tongues. They knew this to be the external manifestation of the presence of the holy spirit. But when they saw the Gentiles manifest, they were dumbfounded. Here was the proof that these Gentiles had been born again and had received the gift from the Holy Spirit for they heard them magnifying God in tongues as the Spirit gave them utterance.

Verse 47:
[Then Peter said,] Can any man forbid water, that these should not be baptized, which have received the Holy Ghost [*pneuma hagion*] as well as we?

The excitement of the occasion so overwhelmed Peter that he ordered John's water baptism, but he never carried it out for God changed Peter's mind. Peter said, as recorded in Acts 11:16, "Then remembered I the word of the Lord, how that he said, John indeed baptized with water; but ye shall be baptized with the Holy Ghost." Water baptism was not needed nor administered.

Verse 48:
And he commanded them to be baptized in the name of the Lord. Then prayed they him to tarry certain days.

147

Why is it that we have seldom, if ever, realized the great impact of the Word of God in this tenth chapter of Acts? Is it because Satan would keep us blinded to the great truths of God's Word regarding the gift from the Holy Spirit? Peter was a Jew. He would no more think of baptizing a Gentile nor bringing him into the Church than we would think of flying a kite to the moon. But there was something in this incident which was indisputable, something that could not be denied. So immediately after Peter heard them speak with tongues magnifying God, he did not have to put them on probation to determine if they were really born again. He *knew* they were born of God's Spirit, for the only visible and audible proof that a man has been born again and filled with the gift from the Holy Spirit is *always* that he speaks in a tongue or tongues.

This ends the fourth record in the Word of God concerning the receiving of the new birth, the gift from the Holy Spirit by any group or individual. Here, for the first time in the history of the Christian Church, Gentiles received the new birth and the gift from the Holy Spirit into manifestation by the ministry of Peter.

CHAPTER TEN

A Study of Acts 19

A fifth and final record in Acts (the Word of God) regarding anyone's or any group's receiving the holy spirit is in Acts 19.

We have already seen the progressive unfolding of the truths regarding the receiving of the gift from the Holy Spirit in Acts 2 where the twelve apostles received; Acts 8 where "half-Jews," the Samaritans, received; Acts 9 contains the record that an individual, Paul, received, being ministered to by a disciple named Ananias; and then in Acts 10 the Gentiles received. Now we come to the final record in Acts 19.

To understand Acts 19 we must begin reading in Acts 18.

Acts 18:24,25:

And a certain Jew named Apollos, born at Alexandria,* an eloquent man, *and* mighty in the scriptures, came to Ephesus.

This man was instructed in the way of the Lord; and being fervent in the spirit [spiritually fervent or enthusiastically spiritual], he spake and taught diligently the things of the Lord, knowing only the baptism of John.

Apollos was a mighty man in the Scriptures; he was eloquent; he was instructed in the way of the Lord, but only to a limited degree. He knew the baptism of John which was a water baptism, but he did not know about the manifestation of the holy spirit. Apollos journeyed to Ephesus.

Verse 26:

And he began to speak boldly in the synagogue: whom when Aquila and Priscilla had heard ....

Aquila and Priscilla were a husband and wife who had left the city of Rome because of the persecution and had come to Ephesus. There they heard Apollos

*In the early Church age there were two major schools of learning, Antioch in Syria and Alexandria in Egypt. The Greek center of learning at Alexandria, where Apollos lived and was educated, lacked the fullness of knowledge regarding the holy spirit which was known in Antioch and therefore throughout the region including Ephesus.

150

speaking the Word of God.

Verse 26:
... they took him unto *them,* and expounded unto him the way of God more perfectly.

How wonderful that is. Apollos was eloquent and mighty in the Scriptures, yet he was humble enough to listen and learn from these simple disciples as they "expounded unto him the way of God more perfectly." Aquila and Priscilla understood the Word of God even better than Apollos so when they heard Apollos preach and teach the new birth but not the manifestations of the holy spirit, they undertook to explain to him the great truths pertaining to the Holy Spirit and His gift.

Verses 27,28:
And when he [Apollos] was disposed to pass into Achaia, the brethren wrote, exhorting the disciples [in Achaia] to receive him: who, when he was come, helped them much which had believed [in Achaia before] through grace:

For he mightily convinced the Jews, *and that* publickly, shewing by the scriptures that Jesus was Christ.

Apollos had been in Ephesus and talked to them

151

about the Lord Jesus Christ, proving from the Scriptures that Jesus was the Christ. Some of the people had believed. Aquila and Priscilla had expounded the Word of God more perfectly to Apollos and then he had gone to Achaia, specifically to Corinth. While Apollos was at Corinth, Paul passed through Ephesus.

> Acts 19:1,2:
> And it came to pass, that, while Apollos was at Corinth, Paul having passed through the upper coasts came to Ephesus: and finding certain disciples,
>
> He said unto them, Have ye received [*lambanō*] the Holy Ghost [*pneuma hagion*] since ye believed? ....

Paul questioned these disciples who had been won to the Lord and born again under the ministry of Apollos. He asked if they had received the gift, *pneuma hagion* into manifestation when or since they had believed. Here the word "received" is *lambanō*. He knew they had received spiritually, *dechomai*. So Paul asked them, "Have you received, *lambanō*; have you manifested *pneuma hagion*?"

> Verse 2:
> ... And they said unto him, We have not so much as heard whether there be any Holy Ghost [*pneuma hagion*].

152

They had heard about the Holy Spirit who is God; but they had not heard about receiving into manifestation the gift from the Holy Spirit. When Apollos was ministering in Ephesus, he could and did teach only that which he knew and understood, for no man can teach beyond that which he knows. No man can lead anyone beyond where he himself has been led. That is why today many people are born again of God's Spirit but are not manifesting the power from the Holy Spirit. They have not been properly taught. They do not understand. Some do not care to understand, but many of them would walk into this greater light if these "Apolloses," — the leaders, the teachers, the ministers — themselves knew and were able to help others to receive the gift from the Holy Spirit. There are believers today who would have to answer Paul's question as did these Ephesian disciples, "We have not so much as heard whether there be any Holy Ghost."

Verses 3—5:
And he [Paul] said unto them, Unto what then were ye baptized? And they said, Unto John's baptism.

Then said Paul [to these disciples in Ephesus], John verily baptized with the baptism of repentance, saying unto the people, that they should believe on him which should come after him, that is, on Christ Jesus.*

When they heard *this*, they were baptized in the name of the Lord Jesus.

In these verses Paul is questioning the people about the ministry of Apollos. Paul knew they had been born again before he had arrived because he addressed them as believers and instructed them regarding their baptism. But he perceived that there was as yet no outward evidence or manifestation of the spiritual reality and presence of Jesus Christ.

The next verse tells us of Paul's ministry to those disciples.

Verse 6:
And when Paul had laid *his* hands upon them, the Holy Ghost [*pneuma hagion*, with no article in the Greek text] came on them; and they spake with tongues, and prophesied.

Apollos had led these people at Ephesus into salvation, but, not knowing about the manifestations of the holy spirit, he did not know how to lead them into bringing forth the evidence of the holy spirit.

*The forms of the verbs in the text are conclusive as to where we must divide what Paul said from what he did. What Paul says about John's baptism is in the subjunctive mood. When his own action is involved the mood is changed to the indicative mood. It is evident that Paul's name must be mentioned when he begins to act as seen in verse 6.

Apollos had not had this experience himself so his ministry was limited to what he knew.

What had happened to the Ephesians is still happening today. Many people are born again, but they manifest no evidence in the senses world that they are born again of God's Spirit. In other words, they do not operate speaking in tongues, interpretation of tongues, prophecy, word of knowledge or wisdom, discerning of spirits, faith, miracles and healing. These manifestations of the spirit are the external evidence of the new birth — the power from the Holy Spirit.

So Paul laid hands on these new believers. Why did he lay hands on them? By revelation, indicating receiving revelation from God as to what to do regarding these Christians who had not evidenced the gift from the Holy Spirit. Paul laid his hands on them and he received revelation, and the *pneuma hagion* came into manifestation. These disciples who had been so recently born again now received into manifestation the power of the holy spirit for they spoke in tongues. Who did the speaking? They did the speaking. They moved their lips, throats and tongues; they made sounds. The language they spoke was tongues. *They* did the speaking, but *what* they spoke was as the Spirit gave them utterance.

155

Here for the first time in the book of Acts, we have an added manifestation in evidence, namely, prophecy.

Acts 19:6,7:
And when Paul had laid *his* hands upon them, the Holy Ghost came on them; and they spake with tongues, and prophesied.

And all the men were about twelve.

There are only five records in the Word of God regarding any individual or group of people receiving the holy spirit, *pneuma hagion,* into manifestation. All five, of which this is the fifth and final one, are found in the book of Acts, chapters 2,8,9,10 and 19. As we consider these accounts we find tremendous truths to share with God's people.

In each of these records concerning the receiving of the gift from the Holy Spirit, it is specifically stated, or the implication is so clear it cannot be missed, that when people were born again, filled with the holy spirit, *speaking in tongues* was the external manifestation of the internal reality and presence of the gift. In all five of these records this outward manifestation was the proof of the reality of their experience.

156

No one can manifest the power until he has received the gift. The gift of God is the new birth, the receiving of the holy spirit, *pneuma hagion,* which is the work of God who is the Holy Spirit. Once we have received the gift, holy spirit, which is "Christ in you," we have the God-given ability to perform the act of manifesting the gift by speaking in tongues as the Spirit gives us utterance.

There is no Scripture that teaches that when people are born again they do not speak in tongues. The Word teaches just the opposite. The gift of the holy spirit is to be outwardly manifested. It is not the works of man that are to be manifested. A man may be immerséd, go to church, say "Hallelujah," look religious and be devout, but that is not proof that he has been born again and filled with the holy spirit.

It is important to repeat that there is *not one record* in the Bible that teaches that believers who are born again of God's Spirit do not or cannot speak in tongues. Since all records in the book of Acts clearly indicate that it was the will of God for those who were born again to speak in tongues and that they did speak in tongues, then it obligates those of us who call ourselves Christians to believe the Word of God and to carry out His will in these matters. Thus, we too shall walk in the great manifestations of the power of God.

157

Where shall we go but to the Word of God when we want to know the will of God? We cannot be led by what men say nor by what different schools of learning may teach. We must go to the literal accuracy of the Word of God. Wherever the Word of God mentions speaking in tongues, it says that they spoke "the wonderful works of God" or they "magnified God." When a person operates that manifestation of the gift, it is impossible to speak anything other than the wonderful works of God and thereby magnify God. We need to come back to the Word of God. We must not listen and act on the negative, and many times misleading, opinions of people. We must believe and live by the revealed Word and power of God if we are to please Him.

SECTION THREE

This section in this book is of such vital importance that everyone should read and reread it. Not only should those who have been speaking in tongues and manifesting other evidences of the spirit immerse themselves in this study of I Corinthians 12,13,14, but also those who sincerely desire to manifest, as well as those who have questions regarding the manifestations of the spirit.

The confusion of "gifts" and "manifestations" in the early Church made it necessary for God, by way of the Apostle Paul, to set in order the proper usage of not only the *gifts* of God, but also the *manifestations* of the gift of holy spirit, *pneuma hagion*, to be considered in these chapters. All nine manifestations will be noted, but only the three inspiration manifestations will be studied in depth.

CHAPTER ELEVEN

A Study of I Corinthians 12

Chapters twelve, thirteen and fourteen of I Corinthians have caused believers no little difficulty and confusion. This has largely been due to our failure to read these three chapters as a unit. Most of us, I fear, have magnified I Corinthians 13, frequently taking it out of its context, at the expense of chapters twelve and fourteen. We've done this to our own detriment.

Note that the book of I Corinthians was written to the Church.

> I Corinthians 1:2:
> Unto the church of God which is at Corinth, to them that are sanctified in Christ Jesus, called *to be* saints, with all that in every place call upon the name of Jesus Christ our Lord, both theirs and ours.

161

The Church is composed of born-again believers. Therefore, what we find in I Corinthians will be *to* us, and specifically *for* us, at the present time as much as to believers at any time in the Church Age.

Furthermore, the verse quoted informs us that I Corinthians was written to the saints. Who are the saints? According to the Bible, the New Testament saints are the converted, born-again believers who have eternal life.

This verse states that I Corinthians was written to the saints in every place, namely those who call upon the name of Christ Jesus our Lord. We who call upon the name of Christ Jesus as our personal Lord and Savior find that I Corinthians is written to us as well as to those in Corinth.

Thus, I Corinthians 12 through 14 are written *to* the saints in the Church of God, and they deal mainly with the subject of *pneumatikos*, "things of the spirit."

I Corinthians 12:1:
Now concerning spiritual *gifts*, brethren, I would not have you ignorant.

The Greek word for "spiritual" is *pneumatikos*, meaning "that which belongs to, is determined by,

162

A Study of I Corinthians 12

influenced by or proceeds from the Spirit."

The word "gifts" is not in any Greek text; therefore, the King James Version has *gifts* in italics.
Reading the word "gifts" into this verse has caused
great confusion, theological arguments and denominational misunderstandings.

Believers belonging to the household of faith are
specifically instructed not to be ignorant regarding
things of the spirit, spiritual things or spiritual
matters, *pneumatikos*, within the Church.

A literal translation of verse 1 according to usage
would be: "Now concerning matters belonging,
determined, influenced or proceeding from the Spirit,
brethren, I would not have you ignorant," or more
simply perhaps, "Now concerning spiritual matters
brethren, I would not have you uninformed."

Verse 2:
Ye know that ye were Gentiles, carried away
unto these dumb idols, even as ye were led.

A "dumb idol" is made of wood or stone and it
cannot speak. The reason the Gentiles had worshipped "dumb idols" was that this is the way they
had been taught. No one ever goes any further in his
spiritual quest than he is led: he cannot receive

beyond what he believes and he cannot believe beyond what he is taught.

Verse 3:
Wherefore I give you to understand, that no man speaking by the Spirit of God [*pneuma theou*] calleth Jesus accursed: and *that* no man can say that Jesus is the Lord, but by the Holy Ghost [*pneuma hagion*].

The spiritual impact of this verse is unparalleled. Any man, even a sinner, could say with this mouth, "Jesus is the Lord"; but to say it with genuineness, a man must have repented, been born again of God's Spirit, and made Jesus Lord in his life. To really mean that Jesus is the Lord of our lives is to carry out God's orders in obedience in His will, "Speaking by the Spirit of God" is speaking in tongues as God who is Spirit gives the utterance. We believe God means what He says and says what He means; and in this verse The Word says it is impossible for any man to say of his life "Jesus is the Lord, but by the Holy Ghost" — which is by way of speaking in tongues.

In the above verse the King James Version adds the article "the" and capitalizes the word *hagion*, Holy; and *pneuma* is translated "Ghost" with a capital "G." This is unfounded liberty. To add the article "the" is changing the text. Omitting the article as in all the critical Greek texts, just *pneuma hagion*, it almost explains itself. Our problem lies in our

164

unwillingness to believe and change. Here, *pneuma hagion* is the gift from the Giver. Every place in the book of Acts where the initial external evidence in connection with the receiving of the gift is mentioned, the evidence is always speaking in tongues. Thus, by sheer logic the same must apply here for this is not *the Holy Spirit* but simply, *pneuma hagion*, holy spirit, which is the gift.

The believer is to *really* make Jesus Lord. We gladly accept many other points, but this final step is difficult. For when we do make Him Lord, we have to change so much of our thinking and action; and this renewing of the mind is certainly difficult.

Many times "unbelieving believers" have said to me that it is possible to curse God when speaking in tongues since the speaker does not understand what he speaks. This is absolutely not true. The third verse of this chapter plainly states that no one can call Jesus accursed when speaking by the spirit of (from) God. Since it is impossible to speak in tongues except one has received the gift from the Holy Spirit, we can be fully confident that this manifestation absolutely can *never* be perverted to the unthinkable end of cursing God. When a man is born again of the Spirit and speaks in tongues, the language and the subject matter which he speaks originate with God and can do nothing other than glorify His name. Furthermore,

165

"And no one can [really] say, Jesus is [my] Lord"
(the Amplified New Testament) except by way of the
pneuma hagion, which is the gift in manifestation.

Verse 4:
Now there are diversities* of gifts, but the same
Spirit [*pneuma*].

The effects produced are diverse kinds. The Greek
word for "gifts" is *charismata*, meaning "gifts of
grace," from God to man. Here, The Word is talking
about *gifts*, not manifestations. Gifts of God are
"spiritual matters," *pneumatikos*, even as the manifestations are.

There are two major groupings of these gifts of
grace:

1. To believers — eternal life (Romans 6:23).
   a. The ability to manifest the holy spirit.

2. To the Church of the Body — ministries of
   apostles, prophets, evangelists, pastors and
   teachers (Ephesians 4:11).

But it is the same Giver — Spirit, Lord, God, in
every case when a *gift* is given.

*The word "diversities" is the Greek word *diairesis*, a compound word
from *dia* meaning "through" and *haireō* meaning "choice" or "option."
Therefore the literal understanding is *charismata*, gifts, "through God's
choice or option" or "through the choice or option of God there are
gifts."

166

Note that in the genitive case as used here in verse 4, "diversities of gifts," both the "gifts" and "diversities" are the *effects* of God's gracious working.

Verse 5:

And there are differences of administrations, but the same Lord.

God gives different ministries in the Church to benefit those who are both within and without the immediate confines of the Church, all to the glory of the same Lord.

The word "differences," like the "diversities" of verse 4, is the Greek word *diairesis** which is the act of dividing through God's choice or option. This is God's absolute prerogative. "Administrations" is the Greek word *diakonia* meaning "ministries whose services benefit others." This simply proves that the ministries, gifts of God's grace, are to be of service in benefits to others. The *charismata* are divided so that not only are their ministries or services of benefit to others, but also of *profit* to the one ministering.

In essence this verse says that the dividing of the gifts is God's prerogative in order to make the ministries in the Church of the greatest service and benefit to all.

*The word "diversities" is the Greek word *diairesis*, a compound word from *dia* meaning "through" and *haireō* meaning "choice" or "option". Therefore, the literal understanding is *charismata*, gifts, "through God's choice or option" or "through the choice or option of God there are gifts."

Verse 6:

And there are diversities [*diairesis*] of operations [*energēma*], but it is the same God which worketh [*energeō*] all in all.

The verb of the Greek word for "operations" is translated "worketh" in the latter part of this verse and in verse 11, while in verse 10 it is "working." It means "that which is wrought." From this Greek word, *energēma*, we get our English word "energy." The effects produced or wrought are diversities, *diairesis*, or distributed kinds. There are deliberate acts of dividing by God of the gifts, like apostles, prophets, evangelists, teachers and pastors; but it is the same God who energizes all the gifts. God *does not* give nine gifts of the Spirit, but He gives one gift of *pneuma hagion* which energizes our spiritual ability to manifest nine operations, plus energizing the five ministries of service in the Church body.

The nine operations from one source of power is like the battery of my car which stores electrical energy. This electrical energy produces several operations. I utilize the energy by sounding the horn or turning the ignition key or playing the radio or lighting the headlamps or turning on the heater. All these operations are produced by the same energy from the one battery.

Verse 6 clearly states that there are diversities of operations produced, *energized*, by the same God.

168

Perhaps it is asked, "Why then doesn't each spirit-filled person manifest the nine evidences of the spirit?" I ask you, "Why doesn't my car horn start honking as soon as I sit in my car?" The reason is obvious. I must first press the horn button to make the contact; the power or energy is already provided for me to use, but latent until I learn of its existence and then activate it.

In essence this verse says, "Among the gifts of grace which are God-given, there are different kinds of effects produced, but it is the same God who is Spirit and Lord who energizes all the gifts.

Verse 7:
But the manifestation of the Spirit [the *pneuma*] is given to every man to profit withal.

The word "but" sets this verse in contrast with, not in correspondence with, that which precedes. Here in verse 7 we change from gifts to manifestations. We are no longer dealing with gifts, we are dealing with evidences, things manifested. All of God's gifts are spiritual and cannot be seen in the senses world until manifested. We cannot see spirit. The word "manifested" means "shown forth in the senses world or evidenced."

The privilege of manifesting the nine supernatural operations in the Church is determined by the Spirit.

169

The reason the word "manifestation" is in its singular form although there are nine in number is the same reason the word "fruit" is singular, and yet there are nine fruits listed in Galatians 5:22. It is like a cluster of grapes with nine units on it. So we have one gift with nine different manifestations or evidences.

The manifestation of the holy spirit has nine separate yet united parts making up the whole, and the *whole* is given to every man for benefit to himself and for the common good of the Church.

Every spirit-filled believer has the privilege and responsibility of evidencing or manifesting the spirit in the Church for the benefit of all. Notice very carefully that "the manifestation ... is given to every man." Therefore, everyone who is born again of God and thus filled with the gift of holy spirit potentially has the manifestations. Remember, the gift is given to every man, but since the gift is spirit it comes into manifestation only when man believes and acts accordingly. Unless the recipient believes in his ability to operate these manifestations, they will never be evidenced. The recipient must do the speaking in tongues, the interpreting and the operating of the other seven manifestations.

Then note the last three words — "to profit withal." The word "to" is *pros* indicating the

170

ultimate view. It could also be translated "toward" or "for." "Withal" gives the added understanding of superior benefits "entirely or altogether," in other words, immediately *and* ultimately. A literal translation according to usage of verse 7 would be, "But to every man is given the manifestation of the spirit toward profit to him ultimately as well as immediately."

Every manifestation of the spirit is profitable. And profit is gained from the evidencing of every manifestation. That is why I immediately look for the profit when people are manifesting anything which they call spiritual or from God. If what they are manifesting is not beneficial, it cannot be from God who is the Father of our Lord and Savior Jesus Christ and the Giver of the gift of *pneuma hagion*.

Naturally, "to profit withal" leads to a question, namely, how does or how will it profit? What is the profit in each of the nine manifestations? The answer is given in verses 8 to 10.

Verses 8 – 10:
For to one is given by the Spirit [the *pneuma* in the Church] the word of wisdom; to another the word of knowledge by the same Spirit [the *pneuma*];

171

To another faith by the same Spirit [*pneuma*];
to another the gifts [*charismata*] of healing by
the same Spirit [*pneuma*];

To another the working of miracles; to another
prophecy; to another the discerning of spirits
[*pneuma*]; to another *divers* kinds of tongues;
to another the interpretation of tongues.

The first word in verse 8 is "for" which is a
conjunction setting this verse in correspondence with
the profit of verse 7, and informing us that God's
Word is now going to give the specific information to
us as to how this profit comes about.

The words "to one" in verse 8 are one word in
Greek, *hō*, which is the dative case of the relative
pronoun *hos*; being in the dative case this word *hō*
can be translated either "to one" or "for one," and
from the context *hō* should be translated "for one."
"One" is a relative pronoun and is used inter-
changeably with the word "that." A relative pronoun
refers to the nearest noun as its antecedent. Therefore, using the noun in place of the pronoun, the
verse would read, "for that [meaning the profit]."

With this understanding of Greek usage, verses 8 to
10 would be accurate and more emphatic when translated as follows:

For a word of wisdom is given by the Spirit for profit;

And a word of knowledge is given by the same Spirit for another [*allos*] profit;

And faith [believing] by the same Spirit for another [*heteros*] profit;

And gifts of healings are given by the same Spirit for another [*allos*] profit;

And the working of miracles is given by the same Spirit for another [*allos*] profit;

And prophecy is given by the same Spirit for another [*allos*] profit;

And discerning of spirits is given by the same Spirit for another [*allos*] profit;

And kinds of tongues are given by the same Spirit for another [*heteros*] profit;

And interpretation of tongues is given by the same spirit for another [*allos*] profit;

I have noted in brackets that the Greek word for "another" used with the manifestation of believing and kinds of tongues is *heteros*, which is different

173

from *allos* which is associated with the other seven manifestations. Why is *heteros* used twice and *allos* seven times? There must be a reason for the usage of two different Greek words which in all cases are translated "another."

Allos is translated "another" and is accurately used as "another" when more than two may be involved. (See Matthew 4:21; 21:8,36,41.)

Heteros is used for "another" when *only* two are involved.* (See Matthew 6:24 and Luke 5:7.)

Two of the nine manifestations are specifically for only the individual believer to profit. The manifestation of tongues and the manifestation of believing are a profit only to the person receiving from God. Speaking in tongues profits the believer by edifying his spirit. The manifestation of believing, which is shown forth when a son of God believes for the impossible to come to pass at his command according to his received revelation (word of knowledge, word of wisdom and discerning of spirits), profits only the believer operating it. Other people may profit from the result of the operation, but not from the manifestation itself. Since no other person profits from the usage of believing and tongues, *heteros* is used

Heteros may and is used also as a generic discrimination in some instances, but not in this Corinthian section where *heteros* always means "another" in respect to two parties.

174

because two and only two are involved, namely, God and the believer. All the other manifestations may be of profit to others besides the person operating the manifestations.

Verses 8 through 10 are *not* a listing of the nine manifestations of the spirit, miscalled "gifts of the Spirit," in their proper sequence and order of unified manifestation. You will notice that they are specific evidences, operations or workings, as benefits, energized by the Spirit. The manifestations are evidences of the gift from the Holy Spirit. They are *not* the gift itself but the workings thereof. Had God meant "gift" or "fruit," He would have said so. He meant manifestation, therefore, He said so.

The *manifestations are evidences of the gift of pneuma hagion*, holy spirit. The manifestations are nine in number, no more, no less; and all nine are "wrapped up" in the gift of *pneuma hagion*, holy spirit, which is received by the believer at the time of the new birth.

If you study the nine manifestations carefully, you will find that seven of these nine evidences of the holy spirit were in operation at various times throughout Old Testament days — all except speaking in tongues and the interpretation of tongues.

When you view the nine manifestations of the holy spirit available to all believers after Pentecost, you will notice how by their very nature, they divide into three groups with three specific manifestations in each group. The groups are:

I. *Utterance, Speaking, Worship, Inspirational Manifestations* (the names suggest the characteristic of the particular manifestation):

    1. Many kinds of tongues

    2. Interpretation of tongues

    3. Prophecy

II. *Revelation, Information, Instructional, Knowing Manifestations* (the eyes and ears of the Church):

    1. Word of knowledge

    2. Word of wisdom

    3. Discerning of spirits

III. *Action, Power, Impartation Manifestations:*

    1. Faith (believing)

    2. Gifts of healings

    3. Working of miracles

All nine manifestations are energized in every believer by the Holy Spirit, who is God, by way of the indwelling presence of the gift, *pneuma hagion*, the holy spirit. The believer shows forth the power from on high in manifestations by acting upon The Word.

The inspirational manifestations that minister to the individual and are for the benefit of the Church may also be referred to as worship manifestations because these may be employed specifically in public worship. They are also "utterance" or "speaking" manifestations for they are uttered forth or spoken out by the believer as he is inspired.

Divers kinds of tongues, interpretation of tongues and prophecy are the evidences of the holy spirit with which the Word of God is specifically concerned in the fourteenth chapter of I Corinthians. Paul was alarmed about the misuse and abuse of these manifestations in the Church. As a demonstration or evidence of the presence of the holy spirit, the power from on high, the manifestations had to be used properly by every individual at all times.

Verse 11:
But all these [all nine manifestations] worketh [are energized by] that one and the selfsame Spirit [*pneuma*], dividing to every man severally as he will.

177

Verses 8 to 10 are a subordinate clause referring to the profit in the manifestations. These three verses, technically and grammatically speaking, should be a parenthesis in correspondence with verse 7 elaborating on the profit. In verse 11 the Word of God again coordinates verse 7 with the conjunction *but*, which again contrasts the aforementioned profits in verses 8 to 10 and relates verse 11 with verse 7.

There is a unique triple reflective in verse 11 in the words "one and the selfsame Spirit" with the emphasis made by *one, self and same*. Then the word "dividing," *diaireō*, is "distributing."

The last four words of verse 11, "severally as he will," have caused no end of confusion. Some teach that no believer can have more than one manifestation, which they call a gift, as a "gift of speaking in tongues" or as a "gift of interpretation of tongues." Furthermore, some teach that these "gifts" can only be given by God when the believer is "sanctified," holy enough to receive, and that never more than one "gift" is given to a believer. Yet, they say that on very rare occasions it may be possible to have two "gifts" in manifestation.

Frankly, even upon the surface of such statements and teaching, one can readily see great Biblical error. If this were true, then God would be a "respecter of

178

persons," which The Word says He is not (Acts 10:34; Ephesians 6:9; Colossians 3:25).

Those who teach the "one gift" theory do not take into account the latter part of verse 11, "... dividing to every man severally as he will." They say, "God divides to every man severally as He [God] wills." My answer is, how can God's will be changed when His will is so clearly stated in verse 7 that all the manifestations are given to every man? Therefore, "as he will" means "as each man wills."

The word "severally" in verse 11 is the Greek word *idia* from *idios*, meaning "one's own." This is the only place in the Bible where the word *idios* is translated "severally." *Idios* is usually translated "one's own," "his own," "your own." F   instance, "He came unto his own," "his own sheep," "his own country," "his own servants," "his own house."

In II Peter 1:20, *idios* is translated "private"; and if it is "private," it is surely "one's own." The word *idios* occurs 114 times, but not once is it rendered "severally" except for verse 11. This makes its usage in this verse sufficiently abnormal to be suspect. It would be more consistent with the Word of God to translate it as the translators have done at these other places, namely, as "one's own."

Thus, if we translate the latter part of verse 11 "distributing to every man his own," we will have truth instead of error. The expositors have said the

179

phrase "as he will" means "as God wills," implying very succinctly that it is not God's will for a believer to possess and operate all nine manifestations of the spirit. The will of God can be determined only from the Word of God. In verse 7 God specifically set forth His will in stating that the manifestation of the spirit (the *pneuma*) is given to *every man* to profit withal. In other words, all nine manifestations are available to every man; but each person, because of his believing ability, may have a very special adeptness, *genos*, in one of the manifestations in the Church.

Thus, there is harmony between the apparently contradictory concepts of verses 7, 8 and 11. Just another irrefutable proof that the Bible does not contradict itself. Every spirit-filled believer has all nine manifestations, but all nine are not always operative in the same person because he may not believe sufficiently. A believer may have a strong desire to manifest one of the evidences over the others. Then this believer will excel in this as his personal contribution to the body of spirit-filled believers in the Church, even though he effectively operates the other manifestations in his private life. This is a believer's prerogative, "as he wills." God energizes *all* manifestations in *every* believer, but the believer may manifest, in the Church, *one* of the manifestations more effectively according to his own believing for the benefit of all.

This is an astounding reality which agrees with every segment of The Word. God gives the gift which is spirit; but once given, it is the recipient of the gift, namely, the spirit-filled believer, who is responsible for its operation. As an illustration, you may have the strength and the ability to stand on your feet, but you may not will to stand. In other words, to have ability does not necessarily mean that you will utilize that ability. Certainly the laws of God work with as much accuracy as do the physical laws of nature.

The evidences of the gift, the holy spirit, *pneuma hagion*, in the spirit-filled believer in the senses world are according to *each man's* believing. God is more anxious to give than we are to receive. At this point, our believing, not God, makes possible the reality of our receiving into manifestation. God wills these manifestations to be shown forth *now* in every believer according to the man's believing. If a believer does not act, he will never manifest God's gift.

Let us reiterate thus far in I Corinthians 12. Key words found in verses 4, 5 and 6 are the following:

"gifts" – *charismata* – gifts of grace which are God-given abilities, always vertical in relationship to man. *God to man.*

"administrations" – *diakonia* – ministries, ways of

serving, a ministering servant. This is always *charismata* in action applied horizontally. *Man to man.*

"operations" — *energēmata* — effects, workings. Always the effects produced by the inner operation, *energeō*, energized by the Spirit, and as such evidenced in the senses world.

Here is the important truth: *all* the *energēmata* are in *every* person filled with the holy spirit, *pneuma hagion.*

Verse 6:
... but it is the same God which worketh all in all [*ho de autos estin theos ho energōn ta panta en pasin*].

Note the following translations for the latter part of verse 6.

Authorized King James Version — "... but it is the same God which worketh all in all."

Weymouth — "... and yet the same God produces all the effects in every person."

Goodspeed — "... but God who produces them all in us all is the same."

Revised Standard Version — "... but it is the same God who inspires them all in every one."

The Amplified New Testament — "... but it is the

182

same God who inspires and energizes them all in all."

The New English Bible — "... but all of them, in all men, are the works of the same God."

Look again at the first part of verse 11 for addi tional understanding.

Verse 11:
But all these [all nine manifestations of *pneuma hagion* in a believer] worketh [*energeō*] that one and the self same Spirit [*pneuma*] ....

The word "worketh" is a verb form from the same Greek root word as the word *energēmata*, the noun used in verse 10 when it refers to the working of miracles. In other words, the nine so-called "gifts" are not gifts, but are evidences, results, effects, the manifestations of the *gift, pneuma hagion,* produced by the working, *energeō*, of the Spirit, *pneuma*.

A literal translation of verse 11 is, "But all these nine manifestations of holy spirit in a believer are produced and energized by the one Spirit, distributing to every man his own, and in the effects produced, as the man wills."

The word "gifts" in connection with the healing manifestation in verse 9 must yet be studied if we are to accurately understand verses 7 to 11. Since the nine evidences are manifestations of the gift of the holy spirit in a believer, why then is *one manifestation*, healing, called a "gift?"

The word "gifts" is in the plural* in verse 9, teaching us that once God has, by way of the manifestations in a spirit-filled believer, healed a person of a disease, God can, does, and is willing to heal him a second time of the same disease; then it becomes "gifts of healing" to the one healed. When an individual believes to be healed and is delivered of two or more diseases, it is also "gifts of healings," as we see in the Word of God in I Corinthians 12:28.

Of all the nine manifestations of God's mercy and grace, only healing is a "gift," *charisma*. In effect, these gifts are delivered to the person or persons in need of healing by those ministering. An example of this is found in Acts where Peter spoke to the cripple at the Temple Gate Beautiful.

> Acts 3:6,7:
> ... Silver and gold have I none; but such as I have give I thee: In the name of Jesus Christ of Nazareth rise up and walk.
>
> And he took him by the right hand, and lifted *him* up: and immediately his feet and ancle bones received strength.

*The word "gifts" in verse 9 is singular in all Aramaic texts and refers to each healing.

184

You cannot give the "gift of healing" unless you have revelation. Peter and John must have passed the cripple many times as he sat begging, but this was the time for him to be healed. When the "gift of healing" was brought into manifestation, the cripple was healed. Not only was the manifestation of healing in operation here, but the "working of miracles" was also involved for the healing was instantaneous.

We will now proceed to the next section of Scripture in I Corinthians 12 which is an illutration of the first eleven verses.

> I Corinthians 12:12 – 27:
> For* as the body is one, and hath many members, and all the members of that one body, being many, are one body: so also *is* Christ.
>
> For by one Spirit [*pneuma*] are we all baptized into one body, whether *we be* Jews or Gentiles, whether *we be* bond or free; and have been all made to drink into one Spirit [*pneuma*].
>
> For the body is not one member, but many.

*"For" sets these verses in correspondence with verses 7 and 11 progressively. Verse 7 gives the manifestation of the spirit (nine in number) as God's will for every believer. Verse 11 shows the believer will only manifest as many of these available nine as he wills to manifest. Then in verses 12 to 27 the "members" are again as many of the nine manifestations (verse 7) as the man wills to manifest, set in correspondence with verse 11.

If the foot shall say, Because I am not the hand, I am not of the body; is it therefore not of the body?

And if the ear shall say, Because I am not the eye, I am not of the body; is it therefore not of the body?

If the whole body *were* an eye, where *were* the hearing? If the whole *were* hearing, where *were* the smelling?

But now hath God set the members every one of them in the body, as it hath pleased him.

And if they were all one member, where *were* the body?

But now *are they* many members, yet but one body.

And the eye cannot say unto the hand, I have no need of thee: nor again the head to the feet, I have no need of you.

Nay, much more those members of the body, which seem to be more feeble, are necessary:

And those *members* of the body, which we think to be less honourable, upon these we

bestow more abundant honour; and our un-
comely *parts* have more abundant comeliness.

For our comely *parts* have no need: but God
hath tempered the body together, having given
more abundant honour to that *part* which
lacked:

That there should be no schism in the body; but
that the members should have the same care one
for another.

And whether one member suffer, all the members suffer with it; or one member be honoured,
all the members rejoice with it.

Now ye are the body of Christ, and members in
particular.

This entire section, verses 12 through 27, is an
illustration using the human body to present the same
truth that applies to the spiritual body, which has
been set forth in the opening eleven verses of this
twelfth chapter.

Verse 12 and following proceed to show how the
Church is *one body* and every member is complete as
one in that body, but that every believer is a
particular member of the whole body.

187

Verses 28 – 30:
And God hath set some in the church, first apostles, secondarily prophets, thirdly teachers, after that miracles, then gifts [*charismata*] of healings, helps, governments, diversities of tongues.

Are all apostles? *are* all prophets? *are* all teachers? *are* all workers of miracles?

Have all the gifts [*charismata*] of healing? do all speak with tongues? do all interpret?

Verses 28 through 30 are an expression of the truth that every part, every believer, has a specific ministry to perform, but without the *whole body* all the manifestations could not function.

The critical, unbelieving believers have tried to expound this verse mainly to degrade "speaking in tongues." They have said, "Speaking in tongues is the least important, therefore, God put it last." Such "logic" is almost unforgivable. If you should happen to be the last child, the youngest in the family, would that make you the least important? Somebody or something has to be last. Just because something is last in a list does not carry with it the quality of being the least or unimportant. In writings as well as speech we often read and hear, "This is the last and final

188

point, but allow me to remind you it is not the least important" or "Last, but not least." God's Word is no less God's Word in importance simply because something is last. It is equally God's Word. You cannot write two things at once. One must be first and of necessity another must come later. Surely, God's Word needs a more honest survey than that which these critics have given it. Let us examine carefully what verses 28 through 30 teach. They are full of truth and instruction to those who will to learn.

A literal translation of verse 28, according to usage, would be: "So God has placed some in the Church having the ministry of apostles, prophets and teachers. There are some who minister more effectively as miracle workers, some who are very effective in ministering the blessings of healings, some who are very adept in ministering as helps and governments, and some whose ministry is diversity of tongues."

The Greek word for "diversities" is *genos*, meaning "kind." People having a ministry of "diversities of tongues" do not use one tongue exclusively, but rather they are adept at bringing forth a variety of different tongues. This is using tongues in a more comprehensive sense, that is, the sense described by the word *genos*.

Verse 28 is God's plan for ministering in the Church Age, in which age we are living. I know of no passage of Scripture which nullifies this order for the Church of which you and I are a part. As a matter of fact, Ephesians 4:8 through 18 helps to clarify the *charismata*, spiritual abilities, manifested in the senses world as ruling ministries in the Church. Also Romans 12:4 through 8 casts much added light on this misunderstood subject.

Ephesians 4:7 – 18:
But unto every one of us is given grace according to the measure of the gift [$d\bar{o}rea$] * of Christ.

Wherefore he saith, When he ascended up on high, he led captivity captive, and gave gifts [*doma*] unto men.

(Now that he ascended, what is it but that he also descended first unto the lower parts of the earth?

He that descended is the same also that ascended up far above all heavens, that he might fill all things.)

And he gave some, apostles; and some, prophets; and some, evangelists; and some, pastors and teachers;

*Walter J. Cummins, "Gifts of God" (American Christian Press, New Knoxville, Ohio, 1969).

For the perfecting of the saints, for the work of the ministry, for the edifying of the body of Christ:

Till we all come in the unity of the faith, and of the knowledge of the Son of God, unto a perfect man, unto the measure of the stature of the fulness of Christ:

That we *henceforth* be no more children, tossed to and fro, and carried about with every wind of doctrine, by the sleight of men, *and* cunning craftiness, whereby they lie in wait to deceive;

But speaking the truth in love, may grow up into him in all things, which is the head, *even* Christ:

From whom the whole body fitly joined together and compacted by that which every joint supplieth, according to the effectual working in the measure of every part, maketh increase of the body unto the edifying of itself in love.

This I say therefore, and testify in the Lord, that ye henceforth walk not as other Gentiles walk, in the vanity of their mind,

Having the understanding darkened, being

191

alienated from the life of God through the ignorance that is in them, because of the blindness of their heart:

The word "gift" in verse 7 is *dōrea* which is a benefit to the individual. The word "gifts" in verse 8 is the Greek word *doma*. As such gifts, *doma*, they are benefits on a horizontal plane to the Church. The Greek word *charisma* is a gift of God by grace in a perpendicular way and not a *doma*, not a benefit on an horizontal plane unless put to use, put into practice or operated by the believer.

The *charismata*, spiritual abilities, as *doma* gifts are *to* or *for* the Church: apostles, prophets, evangelists, pastors, teachers, for ministering benefits to the body of Christ, thus the perfecting of the saints.

Romans 12:4 – 8:
For as we have many members in one body, and all members have not the same office:

So we, *being* many, are one body in Christ, and every one members one of another.

Having then gifts differing according to the grace that is given to us, whether prophecy, *let us*

192

prophesy according to the proportion of faith;

Or ministry, *let us wait* on *our* ministering: or he that teacheth, on teaching;

Or he that exhorteth, or exhortation: he that giveth, *let him do it* with simplicity; he that ruleth, with diligence; he that sheweth mercy, with cheerfulness.

The verses just quoted are the same *charismata*, spiritual abilities, given by God to man, becoming *doma* ministries in the Church as the believer operates them. Chapter twelve of Romans from verse 4 on, gives the operator and believer specific instructions, not only as to the ministries, but also as to the conduct of his own life.

In Romans 12:4 the word "office" means "function," naturally, on an horizontal level. "All members in the body have not the same function."

According to usage the following verses in Romans 12 should read:

Romans 12:6, "You, then, in the Church, having *charismata*, spiritual abilities and functions, differing according to the divine favor or friendly willingness of God that is given you, if it be a ministry of prophecy, keep busy manifesting by prophesying according to the proportion of your believing."

Romans 12:7, "Or if you have another type of ministry, get busy ministering; or if your ministry is teaching, get busy teaching; or if you have an exhortation ministry, get busy exhorting."

Romans 12:8 should now begin: "He that giveth forth in any ministry in the Church let him do it with simplicity; he that has a ruling ministry, let him do it with diligence; and he that has a ministry making him very adept in mercy, let him do it with cheerfulness." All the instructions following these verses are on behavior, that is, conduct.

Having noted in detail the operation of the ministries and gifts in the Church, we now return to the main chapter under consideration.

I Corinthians 12:29,30:
Are all apostles? *are* all prophets? *are* all teachers? *are* all workers of miracles?

Have all the gifts [*charismata*] of healing? do all speak with tongues? do all interpret?

The literal rendering is, "Not all are apostles, are they? Not all are prophets, are they?" and so on. In other words: "Does every one have in operation the ministry of an apostle in the Church? Does every one have in operation the ministry of a prophet in the Church? Do all have in operation the ministry of a teacher in the Church? Are all those who minister, workers of miracles in the Church? Do all have the spiritual abilities in evidence of ministering gifts of healing in the Church? Do all minister by speaking in tongues in the Church? Do all minister by interpreting what has been spoken in a tongue in the Church?"

The answer is: No, they do not all do all of these things *in the Church*. But, there is no implication or inference that these things could not be happening in the lives of all the individual Christian believers.

But, in the Church you will see in manifestation the ministries where the person ministering is especially adept at doing certain spiritual things better than others. All the ministries in the Church, even those that are "gifts," *charismata* of God in a vertical way, will be in manifestation or evidence on the horizontal plane among the believers in the Church *only* according to the proportion of believing of the individual spirit-filled believer who is ministering. As an illustration: if a man has the ministry of an apostle, it will not come forth of itself in *doma* or benefit form to the Church unless he believes he can minister as an apostle. Likewise, all of God's

195

charismata, which are *dōrea* to the individual and *doma* to the Church as the receiver believes to operate them.

Verse 31:
But covet earnestly the best gifts [*charismata*: in the Church] ....

This instruction compels those of us who belong to the Church to covet the best gifts. The word "covet" means "to earnestly desire and seek" the best gifts, with all our heart, soul, mind and strength, that we may have the power of God in our lives to minister effectively in the Church against the onslaughts upon the Church of Jesus Christ. The "best gifts" referred to are the *charismata*. If we have the ability, it is up to us to launch out into the ministry. If we do not have the spiritual ability in evidence in the Church we need to do some earnest desiring.

What are the "best gifts," *charismata?* The word "best" has confused us to the end of thinking that one gift of God might be better than another. This cannot be, for every gift of God is "very good," yes, perfect. But what would be the "best" gift of God for one local church might not be the "best" for another group of believers in another local church. For instance, if one church fellowship should be located in an area among many who are unsaved, then that church fellowship should "covet earnestly the best

196

gift" of an evangelist. Another church in another area may be located among Christian believers only. This church does not need an evangelist; this church should "covet earnestly the best gift" of a pastor. Remember this verse deals with *charismata*, gifts of God's grace, gift ministries of apostles, prophets, evangelists, teachers and pastors.

I Corinthians 12:31:
But covet earnestly the best gifts: and yet shew I unto you a more excellent way.

A more excellent way than what? A more excellent way than coveting or earnestly desiring these gifts, *charismata*. This *better way* than coveting is the way that is set forth in the thirteenth chapter. We will see as we study this chapter that, if and when we apply the principles of the love of God in the renewed mind in manifestation in our lives, we will no longer need to "covet" or "earnestly desire" anything, for God knows our every need and He will supply to us most liberally, even before we ask.

According to usage, verse 31 should read: "But earnestly desire to operate in the Church the best gifts, *charismata*, and yet I will show you a more excellent way than coveting them."

CHAPTER TWELVE

A Study of I Corinthians 13

Before we begin a discussion of I Corinthians 13, let me explain to you the word "charity" which appears in the King James Version, as a translation of the Greek word *agapaō*. There are two Greek words in the Bible for love:

1. *phileō* — natural or human love.
2. *agapaō* — divine or God love.

Any unsaved sinner may have *phileō* love but not *agapaō*. *Agapaō* love is possible to believers only. The love of God, *agapaō* comes into the born-again man at rebirth. If the mind is renewed, and "we walk in the light, as he is the light," then this new kind of love will be manifested in the world. The thirteenth chapter of I Corinthians refers only to *agapaō* love called charity in the KJV, which is the love of God in the renewed mind of the believer in manifestation. It

199

is the "active" love of God. From God's vantage, *agapao̅* is a gift to man, and as such it is spiritual. The "love of God" in the inner man is from God at the time of the new birth, and must be clearly distinguished from, and not confused with, the love of God in the renewed mind in manifestation. This confusion has caused no end of useless conflict.

Everything we receive from God is of grace. Anything man does, or can do, is works and not grace. When *agapao̅* is manifested, it must be by the renewed mind which takes intentional effort. Therefore, since the whole of this chapter deals with what man does, which is works, the word *agapao̅* must be understood as "the love of God in the renewed mind in manifestation." (See Romans 12:2; 13:14; Ephesians 4:23; Philippians 2:5; Colossians 3:5 − 17.)

> I Corinthians 13:1:
> Though I speak with the tongues of men and of angels, and have not charity [love of God in the renewed mind in manifestation], I am become *as* sounding brass, or a tinkling cymbal.

All of the nine manifestations of the holy spirit, as well as all gift ministries, operate effectively and rightly for the individual believer's profit, only as they are operated with the love of God in the renewed mind in manifestation. This verse does not say

200

that the speaking in tongues itself, operated outside of love, becomes nothing. It says, "I am [the person is] become *as* sounding brass, or a tinkling cymbal." Without renewing his mind with the love of God, the manifestation profits *him* nothing because it is love that makes the manifestation really worth while to the operator in practice. A man outside of love, even though he may speak with the tongues of men and of angels, *he*, not the manifestation, becomes as sounding brass or a tinkling cymbal because *he* fails to manifest the love of God in his renewed mind. It is always the will of God for the person ministering to profit even as the ones ministered to must profit also.

A person speaking in a tongue will always be speaking a tongue of men or of angels. If he speaks a tongue of men, it is a known language somewhere on earth; if he speaks a tongue of angels, it cannot be a known language anywhere on earth.

Verse 2:
And though I have *the gift of* prophecy, and understand all mysteries, and all knowledge; and though I have all faith [believing], so that I could remove mountains, and have not charity [love of God in the renewed mind in manifestation], I am nothing.

The words "the gift of" are in italics; they have been added by the translators and must be deleted, for

201

it is referring to the manifestation of prophecy. It is not the manifestation of prophecy, nor understanding of mysteries, nor knowledge, nor believing that becomes nothing; it is the individual, operating the manifestations without the love of God in the renewed mind who becomes nothing. "... I am nothing." This applies to all nine of the manifestations of the holy spirit as well as all gift ministries. The *gift* is not affected by a man; the gift is perfect for God gave it. But man does not bring profit or benefit to himself unless he operates in love.

> Verses 3 − 8:
> And though I bestow all my goods to feed *the poor*, and though I give my body to be burned, and have not charity [love of God in the renewed mind in manifestation], it profiteth me nothing.
> Charity [love of God in the renewed mind in manifestation] suffereth long, *and* is kind; charity [love of God in the renewed mind in manifestation] envieth not; charity [love of God in the renewed mind in manifestation] vaunteth not itself, is not puffed up,
> Doth not behave itself unseemly, seeketh not her own, is not easily provoked, thinketh no evil;
> Rejoiceth not in iniquity, but rejoiceth in the truth;

Beareth all things, believeth all things, hopeth all things, endureth all things.

Charity [love of God in the renewed mind in manifestation] never faileth: but whether *there be* prophecies, they shall fail; whether *there be* tongues, they shall cease; whether *there be* knowledge, it shall vanish away.

This last verse does not say that prophecies and tongues ceased with the days of the apostles any more than it says that knowledge ceased. The eighth verse clearly states that the love of God in the renewed mind in manifestation never faileth.

Any sensible person knows that there is knowledge in the world today. It has not vanished away. If knowledge has not vanished, then the manifestations of tongues and prophecy have not ceased either. If tongues have ceased, as some claim, then knowledge has also vanished away. Pray tell, how could a person know tongues had ceased if knowledge had vanished away? How ridiculous!

Verse 9:
For we know in part, and we prophesy in part.

It is absolutely impossible, even with the operation of the holy spirit manifestations and gift ministries, for any one person or group of persons to prophesy everything. What we prophesy is always specific, geared to the need of the believers at that particular moment in time and place. Tomorrow's need may be different and the word from or for God then will also change to fit the varied need.

Verse 10 is a systematic and logical conclusion to verse 8.

> Verse 10:
> But when that which is perfect is come, then that which is in part shall be done away.

"But when that which is perfect is come," is said by some to mean when the Bible was given as God's Word. But in context it speaks of seeing Him "face to face," which can only be when the Perfect Lover, who is Christ, has returned. Until the time the manifestations of the holy spirit and the gift ministries will all be operated by believers. They will profit the individual who uses them with his mind renewed and manifesting the love of God, and they will bring great goodness and power to believers in the Church. But, when Jesus Christ has come again, then that which we have been doing in part — namely, the manifesting of the holy spirit, *pneuma hagion*, in us for the protection and the advancement of the Church — will then, and not until then, be done away with; and

204

rightly so, because when Jesus Christ comes again, we will not need the manifestations. *We will have Him and be like Him.*

Verses 11 — 13:
When I was a child, I spake as a child, I understood as a child, I thought as a child: but when I became a man, I put away childish things.

For now we see through a glass, darkly [We will continue to see through a glass darkly until Christ comes again.] ; but then face to face: now I know in part; but then shall I know even as also I am known.

And now abideth faith, hope, charity [love of God in the renewed mind in manifestation], these three; but the greatest of these *is* charity [the love of God in the renewed mind in manifestation in the individual Christian and, thus, in the Church].

We are like children now. We need "toys" and the manifestations of the spirit are like spiritual toys to spiritual children. But when He comes, "childish things" will no longer be needed, for we will see Him face to face and be like Him. But until His return, all nine manifestations of the spirit and all five gift ministries will be in operation among believers.

This thirteenth chapter teaches *how* the manifestations (I Corinthians 12:7—10) and gift ministries (Ephesians 4:11) bless the operators in their usage. Most believers have lauded this thirteenth chapter of I Corinthians, casting doubtful, if not disparaging eyes, upon the chapters preceding and following. This must never be done if we believe the Word of God to be the Will of God. This chapter is "sandwiched" in between chapters twelve and fourteen and never can be taken out of its context, its sequential order, if we are to properly interpret it and "rightly divide" the Word of Truth to the end of having the true Word.

CHAPTER THIRTEEN

A Study of I Corinthians 14

This fourteenth chapter of I Corinthians is the only chapter in the entire Bible discussing the use and misuse of the worship manifestations of the Holy Spirit's gift of *pneuma hagion*, holy spirit, in the Church.

The worship manifestations are three in number: speaking in tongues, interpretation of tongues and prophecy. These three manifestations may be used in a believers' meeting, bringing edification, exhortation and comfort to the Church. This fourteenth chapter deals almost exclusively with the proper order and usage of these manifestations.

The Church in Corinth had been misusing these manifestations, and thus God, by Paul, puts them back into proper order and usage in this chapter. I want you to note and to be aware of the exact words that are used throughout.

207

I Corinthians 14:1:
Follow after charity [love of God in the renewed mind in manifestation in the Church], and desire spiritual *gifts* [supernatural manifestations], but rather that ye may prophesy [in the Church].

We are specifically instructed that in the Church we are to follow after love, for the love of God in the renewed mind must be in manifestation among the believers to bless all members of the Body of Christ. We are to yearningly desire (the Greek word for "desire" is *zēloō*. jealous zeal) spiritual or supernatural manifestations. We are to hunger after them and put forth an effort to evidence all the spiritual manifestations belonging to, determined by, influenced by or proceeding from the Spirit. The word "gifts" is in italics and we discussed this previously in I Corinthians 12:1 as being inaccurate. "Gifts" must be deleted from this verse.

When it comes to a believers' meeting in the Church, the most desired manifestation in practice is prophecy. This manifestation of the holy spirit is not that which the Bible refers to as the office of a prophet. That is something entirely different. The manifestation of prophecy is bringing forth in the language of the majority of the people in the Church a message direct from God or for God which will build up or edify, exhort and comfort the body of the

208

saints. Prophecy will always do one or more of these, and it will always flow with the Word of God, never at cross-purposes to it.

The Word says, "Desire spiritual *gifts* [*pneumatikos,* spiritual things], but rather that ye may prophesy." Why is prophecy here preferred above other "spiritual matters or things?" Prophecy* builds up, edifies, by *forthtelling*, exhorting and comforting. If all in the Church are "fully instructed" which is our greatest goal and desire, *then* naturally God would "rather that ye may prophesy." Therefore, prophecy is preferred in the Church, which would indicate a "fully instructed" body of believers.

The word "rather" is the comparative adverb of the Greek word *mala* and means "more and more."† *Mala* used with *de* reads, "more properly." This word augments the preceding. It does not degrade or negate.

*A man of God operating the ministry of a prophet may forthtell or foretell. The forthtelling is his operation of the *manifestation* of prophecy. His foretelling is the operation of the *ministry* of a prophet. A prophet always has the possibility of both. The prophecy manifestation by a prophet has the same characteristics sense-knowledgewise as by any other believer. However, the ministry prophecy of a prophet would not be by inspiration, but by revelation, and therefore could have foretelling. To the believer both the manifestation of prophecy and the ministry of prophecy would naturally sound the same sense-knowledgewise, but the difference can be known by the content of the message.

†Romans 8:34: "Who *is* he that condemneth? *It is* Christ that died, yea rather, that is risen again, who is even at the right hand of God, who also maketh intercession for us."
Galatians 4:9: "But now, after that ye have known God, or rather are known of God, how turn ye again to the weak and beggarly elements, whereunto ye desire again to be in bondage?" The word "rather" in these two verses is the same Greek word *mala*.

209

The word "that," *hina*, introduces a purpose clause — prophecy in the Church.

A literal translation according to usage of I Corinthians 14:1 would be: "Follow after the love of God in the renewed mind in evidence in the Church, and by doing this you will yearningly desire supernatural manifestations in the Church, and more properly prophecy will be brought forth in the Church."

> Verse 2:
> For he that speaketh in an *unknown* tongue speaketh not unto men, but unto God: for no man understandeth *him*; howbeit in the spirit [*pneuma*] he speaketh mysteries.

The Word of God clearly defines speaking in a tongue. First of all, let us be clear that tongues is unknown to the speaker. The translators of the King James Version put the word "unknown" in italics indicating that it was added to the text to clarify the meaning.

The word "speaketh" is the Greek word *laleō* meaning "using the voice without reference to the words spoken." The man speaking in a tongue does not understand what he is speaking. If he understood, it would not be tongues but a known language to the speaker. For instance, if English is your only known language, and under the inspiration of the Holy Spirit you speak in a language unknown to you, then you are speaking in a tongue.

Speaking in tongues is man speaking what the Holy Spirit has to say, which bypasses the understanding of the man speaking. Not the mental faculties, but the spirit in the speaker is edified. When a man speaks in tongues he is not speaking to men but to God. This does not negate the truth that the total message — tongues with interpretation in the Church — is going to be a message from God or for God to the people. Some may say that it is the man talking to God only. Let me ask you a question. When you say you spoke to your neighbor on the telephone, what do you mean? You mean that when you spoke to him, he also talked to you. You did not do all the talking. This truth here in The Word is the same. Speaking in tongues is God's gift to you, holy spirit, in direct communication with God.

The word "understandeth" is the Greek word *akouō*. meaning "to hear," which in this instance is a figure of speech known as an idiom. In Acts 9:7 they heard the sound of the voice, where *akouō*, "hear," is followed by the genitive case, while in Acts 22:9, "heard" is followed by the accusative case indicating that they did not hear the subject matter spoken, only the voice.

211

The word "him" is in italics and if read in the verse throws the whole Word of God out of order. For, on the day of Pentecost the apostles spoke in tongues and the hearers understood every word. If we omit the word "him" we have the word of God. "... For no man understandeth ..." *akouō*; he hears the sound but the man speaking in a tongue does not understand what he himself is speaking. If he understood it, it would not be tongues but a known language to the speaker.

As a believer speaks in a tongue, he speaks mysteries and the word "mysteries" means "divine secrets." Speaking in tongues is the holy spirit in a believer in direct communication with God by the operation of the free will of the believer. Is there anything more wonderful than for a believer to be able to speak divine secrets? Speaking in a tongue is speaking unto God.

A literal translation according to usage of verse 2 is: "He who uses his voice without reference to the words spoken is speaking in a tongue and is absolutely not speaking to human beings but to the Father. For no one speaking in tongues hears his own speaking to the end of understanding with his mind what he speaks; for in the spirit he speaks with his mouth divine secrets."

212

Verse 3:

But he that prophesieth speaketh unto men *to* edification, and exhortation, and comfort.

Inside the Church where the born-again believers are meeting together, The Word says that prophecy, which is in the language of the majority of the people, will *edify, exhort* and *comfort.*

Prophecy is a supernatural manifestation operated by the believer. The word "speaketh" is *laleō,* explained in verse 2. "Edification" is the Greek word, *oikodomē,* meaning "the act of building men up by way of exhortation and comfort." "Exhortation" is the Greek word *paraklēsis,* which is "appealing to men in a manner of instruction or entreating." "Comfort" is the Greek word *paramuthia,* which is "to speak tenderly or with soft voice so as to heal the hurts and wounds." Thus, prophecy builds up the believers in the Church by way of exhorting and comforting them.

A literal translation according to usage of verse 3 is: "But he that prophesies, using his voice without reference to the words spoken, speaks to human beings building them up by exhortation and comfort."

Verse 4:

He that speaketh in an *unknown* tongue edifieth

213

himself; but he that prophesieth edifieth the church.

Speaking in tongues is the only manifestation of the *pneuma hagion*, holy spirit, mentioned in the Bible which builds up the individual who is speaking, not in his mind or understanding, but in his spirit.

There is a basic law involved here, namely: as the physical body must be fed on physical food, so the spirit in a believer must be fed on spiritual food. Speaking in tongues builds up, feeds, the spirit in the believer. However, wherever believers are meeting, the primary need is the strengthening of the entire body, not the individual alone. Therefore, he who prophesies, edifies the believers, not in the spirit but directly in the renewed mind.

A literal translation according to usage of verse 4 is: "He who speaks in tongues uses his voice without reference to the words spoken, thereby building himself up in his own spirit, but he who prophesies performs the act of building up the Church."

Verse 5:
I would that ye all spake with tongues ....

Here is a direct command of the Word of God to the Church. He desires that all believers speak in tongues. If this is not God's will for believers, then how can any other verse of the Bible be God's will?

214

To speak in tongues is to speak to God, to speak divine secrets, to be edified.

... but rather that ye prophesied ...

Where? In the Church. Why? Because prophecy is the bringing forth of a message in the language of the majority of the people present as it is given by direct inspiration from God and all believers would be fully instructed and understand this.

... for greater *is* he that prophesieth ...

Why? Because tongues without interpretation builds up the speaker only. However, prophecy, being in the language of the people, builds up the entire Church by way of the exhortation and comfort it brings to all the believers.

... than he that speaketh with tongues ...

Because speaking in tongues without interpretation edifies only the spirit of the individual who is doing the speaking.

... except he interpret, that the church may receive edifying.

When the message in tongues is interpreted it will be in the language of the body of the people present. It will build up the Church by edifying the believers.

The word "interpret" is the Greek word *diermēneuō* meaning to "expound" or "make plain" (Luke 24:27; Acts 9:36).

A literal translation according to usage of verse 5 is, "I desire that ye all use your voice without reference to the words spoken, and speak in tongues, but I desire more that ye prophesy, for greater is the measure of quality of prophecy, than of speaking in tongues, except tongues be interpreted, made plain, in order that the Church may receive building up."

> Verse 6:
> Now, brethren, if I come unto you speaking with tongues [in the Church without interpretation], what shall I profit you, except I shall speak to you either by revelation, or by knowledge, or by prophesying, or by doctrine?

There is no profit in speaking in tongues in the Church except the speaker give the interpretation. Therefore, without interpretation I am not building up all believers and, consequently, I am not ministering effectively to all members of the Church. In a believers' meeting everything that is done must be for the profit of all. Speaking by revelation, by knowledge, by prophesying or by doctrine, employs the language of the body of believers present and thus all are blessed.

A literal translation according to usage of verse 6 is: "Now, brethren, if I come to you speaking in tongues, what shall I profit you, unless I speak to you that which has been given to me by revelation knowledge from the Spirit, or in that which would be given

216

by way of a message in prophecy, or I speak to you concerning how to believe rightly?"

In a believers' meeting where the love of God in the renewed mind is in manifestation, whatever is done will be done for the benefit of all. Each believer must be edified, and this could not be done if one person were to speak in tongues throughout the entire meeting. The speaker would be edified, but what about the body of believers? Used in this way the manifestation would be out of place, for love would not be the motivation; if love were the motivating factor, the speaker would be concerned not only about his own edification, but also about the building up of the entire Church.

Verse 7:
And even things without life giving sound, whether pipe or harp, except they give a distinction in the sounds, how shall it be known what is piped or harped?

Unless what is spoken in tongues is interpreted in the Church, all the believers in the Church will not be built up.

Verses 8 – 11:
For if the trumpet give an uncertain sound, who shall prepare himself to the battle?

217

So likewise ye, except ye utter by the tongue words easy to be understood, how shall it be known what is spoken? for ye shall speak into the air.

There are, it may be, so many kinds of voices in the world [*voices* equals tongues], and none of them [none of these voices which are spoken forth in tongues] *is* without signification.

Therefore if I know not the meaning of the voice, I shall be unto him that speaketh a barbarian [If I do not understand the language the believer is speaking, I am unto him a barbarian or a foreigner.], and he that speaketh [in an unknown tongue if it is not interpreted] *shall be* a barbarian [foreigner] unto me.

Thus far The Word has said, "I would ye all spake in tongues," but speaking in tongues in the Church must be interpreted. If it is not interpreted, The Word says speaking in tongues is as though a man would stand in an English-speaking congregation and speak in some foreign language. As far as the people in that particular Church would be concerned, the speaker would be a foreigner, and they could not understand what he said unless someone were present who knew that language and would interpret it in English. Inside the Church everything must be done for the building up of all believers.

Note carefully that basically this fourteenth chapter of I Corinthians deals only with three manifestations of the spirit: speaking in tongues, interpretation of tongues and prophecy in the Church. Whatever is done *in the Church* must be done for the benefit of all. Speaking in tongues in a believers' meeting must always be interpreted that all may be blessed.

Verse 12:
Even so ye, forasmuch as ye are zealous of spiritual *gifts*, seek that ye may excel to the edifying of the church.

Paul says nothing against spiritual manifestations, or speaking in tongues; but in the Church where believers are meeting, the primary task and duty is to excel in *all* spiritual matters and to employ those manifestations which will edify, build up, the members of the entire fellowship.

"Zealous" is the Greek word *zēlotēs*. Note the explanation under verse 1. The word "gifts" is again in italics and in this case must be deleted because we are not studying gifts in the Church, but manifestations. "Excel" in the Greek is "abound." "To" is the Greek preposition *pros*, which governs three cases: genitive, dative and accusative. In the accusative case its usage is "with a view to" anything as an end, in other words, "to the end of" building up the Church.

219

A literal translation according to usage of verse 12 is: "So ye also since ye are so zealous to manifest the supernatural in the Church, seek to abound to the end of building up the Church."

Verse 13:
Wherefore let him that speaketh in an *unknown* tongue [in the Church] pray that he may interpret [in the Church].

If man is going to speak in a tongue in the Church, he is to believe to interpret what he has spoken; not pray the interpretation, but pray to speak the interpretation so that the entire congregation may be edified. "To pray" equals "to believe."

Note all of these verses very carefully. Paul is here specifically speaking to those in the Church, telling them that since they are so zealous for all spiritual matters, they must seek to edify the Church, thus when they speak in tongues they should also believe that they may interpret.

A literal translation according to usage of verse 13 is: "On this very account let him that uses his voice without reference to the words spoken, speaking in tongues, interpret in order that he may build up the Church."

Verse 14:
For if I pray in an *unknown* tongue, my spirit prayeth, but my understanding is unfruitful.

In this verse Paul is no longer speaking about believers in the Church, but he is speaking about himself. He also changes from the usage of "speaking in tongues" to "praying in tongues." The Word clearly says, "if I pray ...." In other words, he, the person speaking, does the praying. What he prays is not of his choosing, but the fact that he prays in tongues is his choice. The believer's freedom of will makes it possible for him to speak in tongues at will. It is his part. "My spirit [*pneuma*] prayeth ...." When we pray in a tongue it is our spirit, *pneuma*, that prays. Thus, we are the ones who are doing the praying. The language or the tongue in which we are praying is unknown to us; it is a supernatural, God-given language. The fact that we pray in the spirit is a matter of *our wills*. "I pray." He, Paul, does the praying, not the Holy Spirit.

Praying in tongues is prayer and praise to God according to my will to do so. It results in feeding my spirit, but furnishes nothing to my mind. The mind is built up by putting the Word of God in it; spirit is built up by Spirit, that is speaking in tongues.

"Understanding" is the Greek word *nous*, meaning "mind." "Unfruitful" means "furnishes nothing." The word "if" implies that I may or may not choose to speak. I, by my will, determine either to pray in tongues or not to pray.

221

A literal translation according to usage of verse 14 is: "For if I choose or will to pray and praise God in a tongue, my spirit prays to God, but my mind gains nothing."

Verse 15:
What is it then? I will pray with the spirit, and I will pray with the understanding also: I will sing with the spirit, and I will sing with the understanding also.

Paul cannot be speaking of the use of tongues in the Church. If he were he would have said, "I will pray with the spirit *and interpret* and I will pray with the understanding also: I will sing with the spirit *and interpret* and I will sing with the understanding also."

"I will pray with the spirit," means, he will, by the freedom of his will, choose to continue to pray with the spirit, which is to pray in tongues. The Word clearly tells how this praying with the spirit is done. Paul himself will do it. He, using his will, determines that he will pray with the spirit, and by his own volition he will pray in tongues.

"I will pray with the understanding also" means that he will, by the freedom of his will, choose to pray in his own tongue, which is to pray with his understanding. Paul makes it clear that he can choose the medium of prayer he wishes to use, for both are

222

under the control of his will and accomplished by his own volition.

"I will sing with the spirit [*pneuma*]" means he will decide and desire to sing in tongues, and adds, "I will sing with the understanding also." Thus, Paul indicates that he will sing in a tongue, bypassing the understanding; and he will sing in his own tongue, or with his understanding, also. This verse answers the question which is sometimes asked, "What about this speaking and singing in the spirit?" Paul used them both, but he did not sing or speak in tongues in the Church unless interpretation followed.

A literal translation according to usage of verse 15 is: "What about all of this then? I will by my freedom of will decide to pray to God in the spirit and I will pray to God with my mind also. I will make melody to God in the spirit and I will make melody to God with my mind also, in my private life."

Verse 16:
Else when thou shalt bless with the spirit, how shall he that occupieth the room of the un-learned say Amen at thy giving of thanks, seeing he understandeth not what thou sayest?

The word "else" equals "otherwise," tying this verse directly with the preceding one regarding praying and singing in the spirit and praying and singing with the understanding. The word "when," *ean*, equals "if."

To "bless with the spirit" is to pray in the spirit or in tongues. How can anyone else in the room with me say "amen" to my "giving of thanks" as I "bless with the spirit" if he does not know what is said? Therefore, referring here to the people again, Paul is saying that they should pray with the understanding and not with the spirit if someone else is present.

The "unlearned" are those who are born again, but have not yet learned to walk by the Word of God because they lack instruction. The "unlearned" are uninstructed. The word "bless" equals "praise God."

A literal translation according to usage of verse 16 is: "Otherwise, if you by your will choose to praise God with the spirit by praying or singing in tongues, how shall he who fills the position of the personally unlearned in understanding the significance of tongues say, Amen, Amen, at thy thankfulness since he does not understand that speaking in tongues is prayer or praise to God?"

Verse 17:
For thou verily givest thanks well, but the other is not edified.

To pray in the spirit, bless in the spirit, is "giving thanks well"; but if anyone else is present it is of no value to him: he is not edified.

Verse 18:
I thank my God, I speak with tongues more than ye all.

This cannot be in the Church, for in the Church tongues must always be interpreted. Paul here specifically says that he speaks in tongues often. If the great Apostle Paul was so blessed and built up by speaking in tongues, maybe we need to do it also. Or have we reached spiritual heights and revelations beyond those of the greatest of the apostles? If "God is no respecter of persons," and it is the will of the Lord that "all speak in tongues," then speaking in tongues must be important for us. In the second verse of this chapter we are told, "For he that speaketh in an *unknown* tongue speaketh not unto men, but unto God ... he speaketh mysteries [divine secrets]." Verse 4 states that "He that speaketh in an *unknown* tongue edifieth himself [builds himself up]." This was God's Word and Paul's teaching, and he practiced what he taught. Paul thanked God that he spoke with tongues more than any in the Church at that time. This manifestation of the spirit which Paul used and found so valuable, he wanted other believers to profit by also. Recognizing the problems that had arisen in

225

the Church at Corinth because of the wrong usage of speaking in tongues, Paul goes into detailed teaching on the subject.

Verse 19:
Yet in the church I had rather speak five words with my understanding, that *by my voice* I might teach others also, than ten thousand words in an *unknown* tongue.

Notice that Paul is now speaking directly to the Church. He does not say that he will not speak in an unknown tongue. He has just told us in verse 18 that he wills to speak and does speak in an unknown tongue more than all the others. But when he, Paul, is in a Church where believers are present, he would rather speak five words with his understanding that all who are present might be built up by his speaking, than ten thousand words in a tongue which no one could understand without interpretation and by which no one but himself would be edified. In this verse there is an idiom, an unusual or peculiar use of "words." Here "words" means specifically "sentences."

Notice that in this verse 19 Paul says nothing *against* speaking in tongues in the proper manner and place. But he explains that within the Church it is not the will of God that the people be left with no understanding of the message. Therefore, we see quite

226

clearly that unless a message in tongues be interpreted
to the edification, exhortation and comfort of the
people present, the message should be in the language
and understanding of both the body of believers and
the speaker.

Verse 20:
Brethren, be not children in understanding:
howbeit in malice [evil intentions] be ye
children, but in understanding be men.

Concerning the usage of speaking in tongues and
praying in the spirit or tongues, we are instructed to
grow up and be men. In the understanding of spiritual
things we are to be more mature than children; but in
malice we are to stay like children who have no
malice.

It is interesting and enlightening to notice that a
number of verses indicate that a message in tongues
must be interpreted; but we have no verse saying that
when we *pray* in tongues the message must be interpreted. *All praying in the spirit is speaking in tongues,*
but not all speaking in tongues is a prayer in the
spirit. Praying in the spirit is designed exclusively for
your own private prayer life to build up your spirit.
Speaking in tongues with interpretation is designed
for a believers' meeting as a message from God or
for God to the building up of the entire body, not
in spirit but in their renewed mind.

Verse 21:
In the law it is written, With *men of* other
tongues and other lips will I speak unto this
people; and yet for all that will they not hear
me, saith the Lord.

The apostle is quoting from the Old Testament,
specifically Isaiah 28:11 and 12. The quotation
differs from both the Hebrew and Aramaic texts as
well as the Septuagint. It is accommodated to the
new circumstances by omission of the center section
which was now irrelevant. God has said that men will
speak with other tongues, and that this speaking in
tongues is the rest which "may cause the weary to
rest; and this is the refreshing" for the weary. How
wonderful, and yet even this mighty blessing, in the
presence and in the midst of the people will not cause
them to hearken to the Lord. It should, but it does
not. In this verse we have the figure of speech, *syno-
nymia* — synonymous words having the same meaning
but different in sound, "tongues" and "lips."

Verse 22:
Wherefore tongues are for a sign [in the
Church], not to them that believe, but to them
that believe not ....

This verse is addressed to the Church, and the
Church is composed of born-again believers. Yet, in

the Church there are some born-again Christians who are "unlearned" (verse 16) and are still "children in understanding" (verse 20). They have become members of the Church and have been instructed, but not sufficiently to fully believe. They are "babes in Christ," referred to here as "them that believe not."

"Unbeliever,"* is the Greek word *apistos:* having been instructed but not sufficiently to fully believe.

"Sign" is the Greek word, *sēmeion*: "signs" indicates the significance of the work wrought.

"Unlearned" is the Greek word, *idiotēs*: uninstructed believer, a babe.

"For" is the Greek preposition, *eis*: it governs only the accusative case and indicates motion toward an object with the purpose of reaching or touching it.

"Not" is the Greek word, *ou*, meaning "absolutely not," the same as in verse 2.

Tongues are for a sign in the Church to the unbelievers, those who have been instructed but not sufficiently to believe and walk in the light. To them, tongues are for a sign of the object, design and teaching of a significant work of the Holy Spirit within the Church. This sign is to inspire these un-

*Apeithēs, another Greek word translated "unbeliever" and meaning "fully instructed, but refusing to believe or be persuaded," is not used in this Scripture.

learned Christians to put forth a greater effort to understand and experience this spiritual manifestation; for the ability to speak in a tongue is divinely given for the purpose of direct and intimate communication with God at all times. Therefore, this divine manifestation is a sign to those in the Church who do not as yet fully manifest the mighty working power of God.

Verse 22:
Wherefore tongues are for a sign, not to them that believe, but to them that believe not: but prophesying *serveth* not for them that believe not, but for them which believe.

Prophesying is the bringing forth of a message, divinely given by God, from or for God to the people in the language of the people, which will build up their believing by way of exhorting and comforting the body of believers. Prophecy is a sign to the instructed and practicing believers, the faithful, because of the significance of the work wrought by the manifestation of prophecy.

A literal translation according to usage of verse 22 is: "Speaking in tongues indicates the significance of the work wrought, not to the faithful, those instructed and walking in the light, but to the unfaithful; while prophecy indicates the significance of the work wrought, not to those who are unfaithful, but to those who are faithful — those instructed and walking by the Word of God."

> Verse 23:
> If therefore the whole church [Note the word "whole" includes the faithful, the unfaithful, and the unlearned.] be come together into one place, and all [Note the word "all."] speak with tongues ...

Everyone speaking in tongues at the same time in the Church, without interpretation, has so discredited the speaking in tongues for some born-again Christians that they have refused to believe anything worthwhile or good could possibly come from speaking in tongues or receiving the gift from the Holy Spirit. But note what The Word says,

> ... and there come in *those that are* unlearned, or unbelievers, will they not say that ye are mad?

The unlearned are those who, though born again, have not yet been sufficiently instructed to be transformed by the renewing of their minds. The unbelievers are those who have been instructed but not sufficiently to believe to the end of manifesting. When they, the unlearned and the unbelievers, hear everyone speaking in tongues at the same time, they will indeed say "that ye are mad." The whole Church

231

coming together and all speaking with tongues at the same time, or one after another without interpretation, would constitute a great bedlam of noises with no edification for the entire body. The uninstructed as well as the unfaithful will all say, "You are out of your minds."

Verse 24:
But if all prophesy, and there come in one that believeth not, or *one* unlearned, he is convinced of [by] all, he is judged of [by] all.

If the faithful believers prophesy, all will be edified, exhorted and comforted. Such a blessing will come to the Church that the true believers will be so inspired that their testimony, witness and sharing will instruct the uninstructed. They will indicate to the unfaithful their faults, and thus by examination and inquiry, all the unlearned and the unfaithful will be convinced and come into a realization of the wonderful power and glory of the "one spirit and one mind" body of Christ.

"Convinced," the Greek word *elenchō* is used seventeen times and is translated in the Authorized Version "convince" — four times; "convict" — one time; "rebuke" — five times; "reprove" — six times; and "tell a fault" — one time. Thus it means "to convince by way of loving reproof or rebuke."

232

"Judged," the Greek word *anakrinō*, means "examine to the end of inquiring, not passing judgment."

"Of," the Greek word *hupo*, governs two cases in the New Testament: genitive and accusative. Here, with the genitive, it marks the instrumental agent from under whose hand or power or work the action of the verb proceeds.

A literal translation according to usage of verse 24 is: "But if all (all the faithful are inspired) prophesy and thereby are built up by being exhorted and comforted by a word from or for God, and there is in the meeting one who is instructed but unfaithful, or one who is uninstructed, that one will be lovingly told his faults and examined to the end of inquiring into his difficulty and be helped by all."

> Verse 25:
> And thus are the secrets of his heart made manifest; and so falling down on *his* face he will worship God, and report that God is in you of a truth.

This shows the results of the proper operation of the manifestations of the spirit in the Church — what it will do and accomplish.

> Verse 26:
> How is it then, brethren? when ye come

233

together, every one of you hath a psalm, hath a doctrine, hath a tongue, hath a revelation, hath an interpretation. Let all things be done unto edifying [in the Church].

Paul is saying, "Since you know this, then why is it brethren, that when you all come together in the Church everyone of you wants to have a psalm, and so on? This commotion is as confusing as all wanting to speak in tongues at the same time. During the Church service, we must make sure that all things are done to build up the entire Church body, instead of everyone doing as he pleases."

Verse 27:
If any man speak in an *unknown* tongue [in the Church], *let it* [the speaking] *be* by two, or at the most *by* three, and *that* by course [in order]; and let one [same one or each one]* interpret.

When tongues are spoken in the Church there are never to be more than three messages given, and the interpretation must be given after each message so that all believers may be built up. The one speaking in tongues must always be willing, and believe, to give the interpretation. For note what the next verse says.

*The Greek uses the word *heis* meaning "the one and the same," not someone else. Thus, "let each one who speaks in tongues, that one and the same interpret. I Corinthians 14:5, 13; Luke 12:52; Romans 3:10.

Verse 28:

But if there be no interpreter, let him [who is
speaking or has spoken in a tongue] keep silence
in the church; and let him speak to himself, and
to God.

If the one who desires to speak in a tongue in the
Church lacks either the believing in his ability or the
willingness to interpret what he is about to speak, he
is to remain silent. His lack of readiness to interpret,
either because of insufficient instruction or refusal to
speak forth the interpretation is reason for him to
keep silent in the Church. He may, in that case, speak
silently to himself and to God in tongues, which is
"praying in the spirit." This is private communication
with God, edifying to his own spirit but not to the
Church. It is God's will that all speaking in tongues in
the Church be followed by interpretation in order
that *all* may be edified.

The word "but" in verse 28 again sets this verse in
contrast to the preceding verse where each one
speaking in tongues in the Church is instructed to
interpret.

The words "there be" is in the third person singular, present subjunctive mood; and when "be" is
used with "if," *ean*, they make a conditional clause,
which should be translated literally, "but if he lacks
the will to interpret." The subjunctive mood is used

when the subject of the sentence has doubt or no desire. In this verse the subjunctive usage is, "if he would not will or desire to be an interpreter."

Verse 29:
Let the prophets speak two or three, and let the other [others] judge.

If there are gift ministries of prophets in manifestation inside of the Church, at the most there are to be two or three prophets who speak and the others weigh their messages. The *ministry* of such a prophet will have the same characteristics in evidence as the *manifestation* of prophecy in any spirit-filled believer, with this exception: the prophecy of a prophet is by revelation and not inspiration and will have forthtelling and may foretell that which has not before been told to the believer or believers; but the foretold information will agree with the revealed Word of God and never flow at cross-purposes to it.

For example, Acts 21:10 and 11 tell, "And as we tarried *there* many days, there came down from Judaea a certain prophet, named Agabus. And when he was come unto us, he took Paul's girdle, and bound his own hands and feet, and said, Thus saith the Holy Ghost, So shall the Jews at Jerusalem bind the man that owneth this girdle, and shall deliver *him* into the hands of the Gentiles." The prophet Agabus by

236

revelation foretold what would happen to Paul if he went to Jerusalem.

Verses 30, 31:
If *any thing* be revealed to another that sitteth by, let the first [the prophet who is speaking] hold his peace.

For ye may all [the prophets] prophesy one by one, that all may learn, and all may be comforted.

In the Church every prophet may bring forth a message in prophecy which he has received by revelation, the purpose of which again is that all may learn and be comforted in the Church. For the Church must be edified via the manifestations or direct Word of God as given by the prophet.

According to usage, verses 29 − 31 of I Corinthians 14 could be translated, "Let two or three prophets speak but let the others weigh, evaluate or digest what they are saying. If something is revealed to another prophet who is sitting by, let the prophet speaking be quiet and let the other prophet speak, for all the prophets may prophesy in turn that every believer in the Church may learn and be comforted." This verse is instruction pertaining to the prophecy of a prophet and does not apply to the manifestation of prophecy nor to preaching. The Word means what it says and says what it means.

Verse 32:

And the spirits [*pneumata*] of the prophets are subject to the prophets.

This verse distinctly states that the man is in absolute control of his actions at all times. He can start to speak and he can stop speaking at any time, for "the spirits of the prophets are subject to the prophets." What is said here is applicable to all spiritual abilities and evidences of the holy spirit. Freedom of will is never overstepped as a person operates the manifestations of the holy spirit. The believer is *never* used, controlled, taken over nor possessed by the Spirit of God. God *never* oversteps the free will of man. The believer is not an impersonal channel or instrument. He is a son of God by a decision of his will to believe. Therefore, each believer is responsible for his actions at *all* times; and when he is manifesting any of the spiritual abilities in the Church, all must be done decently and in order for the edification of the whole body of believers.

Verse 33:

For God is not *the author* of confusion, but of peace, as in all churches of the saints.

There should never be any confusion inside the Church, because the Church is the fellowship of the redeemed. It is the fellowship of the believers who are

238

living in love and are banded together in fellowship for their own mutual edification, exhortation and comfort. If there is confusion among the believers — and there will be if the believers do not walk by the revealed Word of God — this confusion is from Satan. (James 3:13 — 18).

> Verses 34 and 35:
> Let your women [the wives of the prophets] keep silence in the churches: for it is not permitted unto them to speak; but *they are commanded* to be under obedience, as also saith the law.
>
> And if they [the wives of the prophets] will learn any thing, let them ask their husbands at home: for it is a shame for women [the wives of the prophets] to speak in the church.

The word "shame" is *aischros* meaning "offensive to modesty, indecorous, lacking in propriety." The implied meaning is that it is just not proper for the wife of a prophet to act thus. "Speak" is *laleo*, "to say words with the mouth without paying attention to what is being said." The wives of the prophets in the Corinthian Church were doing that which no wife of a prophet should have done in public. They were carrying on and thereby degrading their husbands as men of God.

Verse 36:
What? came the word of God out from you [the prophet's wives]? or came it unto you only?

The Word of God was not given by the wife, but by the prophet, for he is the holy man of God who spoke the Word of God as he was moved by the Holy Spirit (II Peter 1:21).

Verses 34 and 35 have caused a great deal of consternation in the Churches which interpret them as saying that all women are always to be silent in the Church. But anyone can see that in their context these verses clearly indicate that "women" can only refer to the wives of the prophets.

Verse 37:
If any man think himself to be a prophet, or spiritual, let him acknowledge that the things that I write unto you are the commandments of the Lord.

Wonderful! There can be no bedlam or confusion if the commandments of the Lord are followed in regard to the operation of the worship evidences from the Holy Spirit inside the Church. The entire fourteenth chapter of I Corinthians is specifically "the commandments of the Lord." It pertains to the mani-

240

festations used in worship, all three manifestations being minutely defined and noting the specific difference between speaking in tongues or praying in the spirit in one's private worship and speaking in tongues in a believers' meeting or when any other person is present. All three of the manifestations — speaking in tongues, interpretation of tongues and prophecy — are inspired utterance, operated by a believer filled with the holy spirit. As you are inspired you give out, and as John 7:38 says, "out of his belly shall flow rivers of living water [not *into*, but *out of*]."

Verse 38:
But if any man be ignorant, let him be ignorant.

Paul says, in effect, "I have certainly, and by commandment of the Lord, clearly set forth the character and use of the manifestations from the Holy Spirit within the Church, the fellowship of believers, and in one's own personal life. Now, if any man still wants to be ignorant after all of this, in spite of the fact that God has said we are not to be ignorant of spiritual things, let the man be ignorant." Nothing can be done if someone does not want to receive and practice the evidences of the holy spirit or does not earnestly covet spiritual things and the proper operation of them in the Church. So let that person stay ignorant and stop fretting about his lack of concern or knowledge. Even though it is the commandment of the Lord, each believer must *will* to receive and operate, otherwise the manifestations will not be in evidence.

Verse 39:
Wherefore, brethren, covet to prophesy, and forbid not to speak with tongues [in the Church].

Paul says that when you are in the Church, your great longing and desire and prayer should be to bring forth a message directly from God or for God to the believers in the language of the people present for the reason set forth in verse 24.

Therefore, who dares to say that there is to be no speaking in tongues in the Church? The Word of God specifically says, "forbid not to speak with tongues." Remember, Paul has before mentioned that in the Church the manifestation of tongues must be interpreted, otherwise the one desiring to speak in tongues must speak silently to himself and to God.

Verse 40:
Let all things be done decently and in order [in the Church].

In verse 33 of the Word of God we are told that God is not the author of confusion. Now this is

242

repeated to emphasize His command for orderliness and to impress upon those who have transgressed the proper usage of the manifestations in the Church: all things must be done decently and in order. God is not a God of confusion; in everything He is a God of order.

I would like now to gather up a few loose threads, reiterating and calling to your attention, first of all, that the manifestations mentioned, including the speaking in many tongues, the interpretation of tongues and prophecy, are inspiration or worship evidences. They are worship manifestations of the holy spirit because of their use in public worship according to the instructions in chapters 12, 13 and 14 of I Corinthians, and they come directly from God by inspiration. These manifestations are also utterance manifestaions which the believer speaks forth as he is inspired, therefore, they are inspired utterance.

The evidence of speaking in tongues is the God-given ability for a spirit-filled believer to speak in a tongue unknown to himself a message to God or, in a believers' meeting, a message from or for God.

The gift from the Holy Spirit is the *same* in all nine manifestations; the gift is the God-given spiritual ability to perform the act. The act varies according to the evidence in manifestation. For example, in the

243

manifestation of tongues, the gift is the God-given ability to speak in tongues; the speaking is the act. In the manifestation of prophecy, the gift is the God-given ability to prophesy; the prophesying is the act; and the same goes for the other five manifestations and the evidencing thereof.

The act of interpretation of tongues is the giving forth in the language of those present, which is also the interpreter's language, the gist, the sum and substance of what has just been spoken in a tongue. The one interpreting does not understand what has been said and does not know ahead of time what words he will be saying. The interpretation is given to him by inspiration as he gives it forth, and the body of believers is edified. *Interpretation is never revelation.*

In the manifestation of prophecy, the gift is the God-given ability to bring forth in the language of the people (your native language), a message directly from or for God to edify, exhort and comfort. The act is your giving forth by your will, in the language of those present, a message from God or for God which has come to you by inspiration and keeps coming as you are giving it forth.

These three worship evidences of the holy spirit in a believer are all operated by inspiration. The believer *never* knows the message ahead of time. Prophecy utterances are *not* premeditated, nor are they thought patterns of the mind. Prophecy always runs parallel to the Scripture and many times it consists of portions of Scripture.

As stated before, tongues is speaking a message from God or for God and must always be interpreted in a believers' meeting. When the believer speaks in tongues or prays in the spirit in his private prayer life, he *never* interprets. Interpretation is the companion manifestation to speaking in tongues which completes it among the believers in the Church. Without interpretation, speaking in tongues is limited to the individual's prayer life, building up himself spiritually.

The twelfth chapter of I Corinthians gives the gifts and manifestations from the Holy Spirit available to the members of the household of faith — the believers.

The thirteenth chapter specifically informs us that these manifestations, as ministries of the holy spirit in a believer, are of no value to the believer if operated outside of renewed mind love. Inside the Church there must always be the love of God in the renewed mind in manifestation, because love is the great keynote of Christian sonship and fellowship.

The fourteenth chapter of I Corinthians gives the particular details concerning the operation of the worship evidences of the *pneuma hagion*, inside the fellowship of the believers.

Paul, under the guidance of the Holy Spirit, set down so beautifully these things in proper order and sequence. Is it not strange that so many of us through the years have failed to see that the thirteenth chapter of I Corinthians follows perfectly after the twelfth, naturally explaining it and preparing us for the fourteenth chapter, in which the operation of the worship evidences within the Church are discussed?

The love of God in the renewed mind in manifestation is the greatest of all. Love is the activating, motivating power behind all *charismata*, gifts of grace. If one had all spiritual things, but did not have love, the individual would become nothing. Spiritual abilities themselves would remain the same. But operated outside of love, the evidences are profitless to the man operating them.

It is wonderful to see how very, very clear the Scripture is and to realize that no man need have any doubts or quirks of conscience or be misinformed or misled. If he wants to read these Scriptures clearly, he can surely understand. But, as the Apostle Paul said, if anyone wants to be ignorant after hearing all this, let him remain ignorant. The hearer now has to make the choice.

246

I know that when I saw the importance of reading these chapters in the light of the Church, inserting the words "in the Church" time and time again, this section of Scripture fit together like a hand in a glove, and it was no longer necessary to explain away one verse or another. The verses all fit together in perfect union, in perfect wholeness.

The Bible is the Word of God; therefore, it is the Will of God. Verses cannot contradict each other and they must always remain in their context to bring forth the message that is there. Whenever one has to remove one passage from the context, we are no longer on the grounds of good Biblical exegesis, because the passages in the Bible must interpret themselves and fit together as a perfect pattern without any additions or subtractions since these words make up the Word of God.

I trust that you are now reading the twelfth, thirteenth and fourteenth chapters of I Corinthians in sequence. Your understanding will take on a new and greater depth of meaning with the result of a new life for you. Will you read it under the guidance of the Holy Spirit, in the light of its own statements? Read it again and again until you, too, have become sure that God means what He says: that the Church today is not to be ignorant concerning spiritual abilities. Then you, too, will see how in most of our Churches today we are certainly missing many of the blessings of God because we have, so to speak, outlawed the presence of the powerful evidences of the gift from the Holy Spirit within the fellowship of the Church. To be fruitful, we must walk in Christ Jesus and God's Word.

CHAPTER FOURTEEN

Some Questions Answered

1. Is the holy spirit available to every believer today?

Yes, indeed. Is the gift of salvation available today? This is not a foolish question. If the gift from the Holy Spirit which is *pneuma hagion*, holy spirit, power from on high, is not available, then neither is the gift of salvation. When God gives a gift, it is here to stay until the Church Age is finished. His gifts are available to and for all believers who *desire* to receive and *know how* to receive.

2. Do I have to tarry in prayer before I can receive the holy spirit?

Definitely not. All of God's gifts — and the holy spirit is a gift — are immediately available by believing

249

to all who will to receive. The Bible does not instruct people to tarry for the holy spirit with the one exception of Jesus' instructing the twelve disciples in Acts.

Acts 1:4,5:
And, being assembled together with *them*, commanded them that they should not depart from Jerusalem, but wait for the promise of the Father, which, *saith he*, ye have heard of me.

For John truly baptized with water; but ye shall be baptized with the Holy Ghost [*pneuma hagion*] not many days hence.

Jesus was instructing the apostles to "wait for the promise" to be fulfilled, before the holy spirit had been given. The Scripture does not say this would happen when the apostles were ready. It says it would be "not many days hence" which, according to Acts 2:1, was "when the day of Pentecost was fully come." Since the outpouring on Pentecost, there is no teaching in Scripture to wait or tarry. I was told by some Christians that if I would go apart alone and pray for ten days, God would give me the holy spirit. I found that God does not wait a certain number of days to give the holy spirit to anyone. He gave the holy spirit once and for all time "when the day of Pentecost was fully come," and the power from on

250

high is immediately available now to anyone who *wills* to receive, and *knows how* to receive.

3. In order to receive the holy spirit, shouldn't all believers be "in one accord" as the apostles were?

No. You can receive the holy spirit in private. It is not necessary for any one person to be present for you to receive. "They were all with one accord in one place" on the day of Pentecost, but this was a unique happening. Jesus had instructed the apostles to go to a specific place and to tarry there until they were "baptized with the Holy Ghost." In obedience to His command they were gathered together in unity of spirit and purpose to wait for the promise to be fulfilled. The instruction was to this particular group at a particular time. Since Pentecost, the common factor in every case for receiving the gift from the Holy Spirit is *believing*.

4. Do I have to be good before I can receive the holy spirit?

No. The holy spirit is never received according to the state of holiness or goodness of Christian character. The holy spirit was a gift, and every gift of God is of grace and is received by believing, not by works. You will have more strength to be good after you have received the gift.

5.   Is the holy spirit for particular or special denominations?

No. The holy spirit is never for denominations as such. The holy spirit is for *believers*. They may come from any or all denominations. People from at least thirty different denominations have received the *pneuma hagion* under my teaching, but not one has received because of his denominational affiliation. They all received because they believed.

6.   Is it possible for one to receive the gift from the Holy Spirit into manifestation without speaking in a tongue?

No, it is not, for the mighty movement from the Spirit will be expressed in *all nine* manifestations from time to time and speaking in tongues is one of these manifestations. Nor would anyone who knows the wonderful Word of God want the gift without speaking in a tongue, for the blessings are innumerable, and it behooves us to follow the commandments of God's Word in all things. The believer who has never spoken in a tongue has failed to do his part in manifesting the gift which has already been given. By the operation of believing he receives through this manifestation the benefit of his own personal spiritual edification.

252

Since Pentecost, there is no record of God's giving the holy spirit to anyone. He gave it once and for all. However, men by an act of believing have *received* into manifestation the spirit which God made available at Pentecost. There necessarily is an *act* to receiving on the part of every believer, and the outward manifestation of having received the gift is the act of speaking with another tongue.

7. Can a person who has received the holy spirit speak in tongues at will?

Yes. The act of speaking in tongues is an act of the will on the part of the believer. He has *the gift*, which is the spiritual ability. Therefore, if he knows what The Word teaches, he can start to speak and he can stop speaking at any time he so chooses.

8. Is it possible for a Christian to receive false tongues or a false spirit when believing for the holy spirit?

The answer is a loud and clear no. As a matter of fact, speaking in tongues is the only manifestation which basically Satan cannot counterfeit. When I am asked that question, I know that person has come into contact with those whom I term "faith blasters," who go about making statements which have no foundation in Scripture. When someone suggests to earnest

Christians that they are in danger of receiving something false when believing to manifest the fullness of
God according to God's Word, he sinfully dishonors
God. Where is there a chapter or verse indicating that
a Christian may get false tongues? It is an unreason-
able idea, for the loving Father cares for His children
and stands ready with His might to protect them from
the power of the enemy. With Scripture as our rule of
believing and practice, The Word contradicts the
wicked thought of false tongues coming from the
Holy Spirit. Luke points out most emphatically that
God will not give His children a worthless or harmful
substitute for the *pneuma hagion*.

> Luke 11:11—13:
> If a son shall ask bread of any of you that is a
> father, will he give him a stone? or if *he ask* a
> fish, will he for a fish give him a serpent?
>
> Or if he shall ask an egg, will he offer him a
> scorpion?
>
> If ye then, being evil, know how to give good
> gifts unto your children: how much more shall
> *your* heavenly Father give the Holy Spirit
> [*pneuma hagion*] to them that ask him?

The very essence of God is love. Can any sane person conceive of a loving Father, who is all-wise and

all-powerful, giving his hungering, believing child a false and harmful substitute? There are hundreds of Scriptures which point out that God seeks only the welfare and blessing of His children.

Cast away forever the repulsive idea that God would allow His child to receive anything false. Pay no attention to anyone who suggests unscriptural doubts or fears.

9.   Why should one speak in tongues when he cannot understand what he is saying?

Paul exhorted all believers to speak in tongues for their edification, and to acknowledge that the things he wrote in his epistles were the commandments of the Lord (I Corinthians 14:4,5,37).

10.   May there ever be any speaking in tongues in public worship?

Yes, but it must always be interpreted. The order and details for speaking in tongues in public worship are clearly given in I Corinthians 14:27 and 28.

11.   Can one person speak in tongues and another give the interpretation?

255

No. We are specifically told in I Corinthians 14:27 and 28 that the person speaking must give the interpretation or else remain silent. Where the practice of one person speaking and another interpreting has been carried on, there is no interpretation of that which is spoken in tongues, but there is prophecy on the part of the so-called interpreter.

APPENDIXES

Introduction to the Appendixes

If we believe that throughout the Scriptures we have the words of God and not of man, many difficulties will disappear. We must allow the Divine Author the rights and privileges claimed and operated by every human author, namely, that He may quote, readapt or repeat in varied forms His own previously written or spoken words. God could have used other forms had He chosen to do so, but it has pleased Him to repeat His own word or words, introducing them in different contexts, with new applications and connotations. Thus it obligates us to study the context, the paragraph and the section where the same word appears and where it was used previously, to see if its usage is in a new sense or not.

The greatest satisfaction of any Biblical scholar is to fathom what can be searched out from His Word and quietly to accept that which is untraceable and cannot be explored or found out.

Ephesians 3:8 — *anexichniastos* — untraceable, unsearchable, cannot be explored or found out. Romans 11:33 uses this same word translated "past finding out."

Romans 11:33 — *anexereunētos* — translated "unsearchable" is simply inscrutable or incomprehensible, which can be apprehended but not comprehended.

This appendix has been added to this volume for those who desire to search out and explore the deeper reason for the way in which God has set truth in perfect order in His Word.

APPENDIX ONE

The Word Receive

Most of the misunderstanding and wrong interpretation regarding the Holy Spirit in the Bible has been due to two things:

1. The capitalization of the words *pneuma* and *hagion*, plus the addition of the article "the" at will by each translator.

2. The misunderstanding of the word "receive." It is "receive" that I want to deal with because it is of utmost importance in "rightly dividing" and understanding the *pneuma hagion* Scriptures.

There are seventeen different Greek word-forms used but all are translated with the one English word "receive." The average student can never see the shades of meaning as given in the Greek, and thus taking "receive" in its commonly accepted sense we develop wrong interpretations.

I believe that to most people the word "receive" means "to take" and that is all. But there are more connotations with this word. Spiritually a person can receive something within the inner man without receiving it into manifestation in the senses world. One can spiritually receive a gift from God without its coming forth in evidence in the senses world; for all of God's gifts are spirit, and, as such, cannot be seen, smelled, heard, tasted or touched. To bring God's gift into evidence we must receive it into manifestation; that is, we must operate the gift.

There are two Greek words that give this difference very clearly: *dechomai* and *lambanō*.

dechomai – receiving from God spiritually within oneself. This is subjective reception.

lambanō – is receiving the gift into manifestation after having received it spiritually. This is an objective reception to the end of manifestation.

In Acts 8:12 the people believed Philip's preaching and in verse 13 Simon believed also. Surely when they believed they were saved and thus "received," *dechomai*, spiritually received, the Lord Jesus Christ,

260

the new birth, for they were "baptized both men and women."

In verse 14 we note that "when the apostles which were at Jerusalem heard that Samaria had received the word of God, they sent unto them Peter and John." This word "received" is *dechomai*, meaning they had received spiritually, but as yet had not manifested anything, that is, had not received into manifestaion. Acts 8:15: "Who, when they [Peter and John] were come down, prayed for them, that they might receive the Holy Ghost." Here the word "receive" is *lambanō*, meaning "receive into manifestation."

Notice the difference in the two usages of "receive." The correct interpretation depends upon understanding the usage of the word as it appears in these verses. In the early Church from the day of Pentecost on, with this one exception, whenever anyone had received salvation he also had received the gift from the Holy Spirit into manifestation. In each case the sign in the senses world that the gift had been received into manifestation was that they spoke in tongues, except in the church of Samaria, where they received the gift spiritually but did not speak in tongues. Peter and John, the two leaders in the new church at Jerusalem, came down to see what was happening there and why. Acts 8:17: "Then laid they

261

their hands on them, and they received [*lambanō*] the Holy Ghost [*pneuma hagion*]." They manifested outwardly what they had previously received spiritually.

In Acts 10:45-47 we are told that while Peter was preaching The Word to Cornelius and his household, the *pneuma hagion* fell upon all of them and Peter and his six companions were astonished that "on the Gentiles also was poured out the gift of the Holy Ghost [*pneuma hagion*]." The reason they knew they had received (*dechomai*) spiritually, was that they now received (*lambanō*) into manifestation, "For they heard them speak with tongues."

In Acts 19:1-6, we have a similar occurrence. Paul arrived at Ephesus and found a few disciples. They were believers, for Apollos had ministered as much of The Word to them as he knew and understood. They had been saved under Apollos' ministry. But when Paul met these new disciples, "He said unto them, Have ye received [*lambanō*, manifested] the Holy Ghost since ye believed?" Later according to verse 6, Paul ministered to them and they received the Holy Spirit into manifestation; for it states that they spoke with tongues.

Thus to "rightly divide the Word of Truth," the usage of the word "receive" is highly important to

262

the proper understanding of the verses of Scripture in which the word appears. In the following pages I have given every reference in the New Testament where "receive" is found, when it is *dechomai* and when *lambanō*, so that you may study the two meanings of the word to your own satisfaction.

Receive is the Greek word *dechomai* — subjective reception spiritually.

MATTHEW
>10:14
>10:40 used 4 times
>10:41 1st and 3rd
>11:14
>18:5 twice

MARK
>4:20
>6:11
>9:37 4 times
>10:15

LUKE
>8:13,40
>9:5,11,48 4 times,53
>10:8,10,38

HEBREWS
    11:17
    11:31
    12:6

JAMES
    1:21
    2:25

III JOHN
    Verse 9
    Verse 10

Receive is the Greek word *lambanō* — objective reception into manifestation or evidence, possible only after *dechomai*.

MATTHEW
    7:8
    10:8,41 2nd,4th
    13:20 2nd
    17:24
    19:29
    20:7,9,10 twice,11
    21:22,34
    23:14
    25:16,18,20,22,24

MARK

    4:16
    7:4
    10:30
    11:24
    12:2,40
    15:23
    16:19

LUKE

    6:34 twice
    9:51
    11:10
    15:27
    16:25
    18:30
    19:12,15
    20:47
    23:41

JOHN

    1:11,12,16
    3:11,27,32,33
    4:36
    5:34,41,43 twice,44
    6:21
    7:23,39
    10:18

8:15 twice
13:2
14:1,3
15:7 twice

I CORINTHIANS
2:12
3:8,14
4:7 3 times
9:24
11:23
14:5
15:1,3

II CORINTHIANS
11:4 twice, 24

GALATIANS
1:9,12
3:2,14
4:5

PHILIPPIANS
4:9

COLOSSIANS
2:6

3:3
4:11
5:12
14:9,11
17:12 twice
18:4
19:20
20:4

APPENDIX TWO

The Use and Usage of the Words Pneuma and Pneuma Hagion

The word *pneuma*, "spirit," is found in the following books.

Book	Number of times used
Gospel of Matthew	19
Gospel of Mark	23
Gospel of Luke	38
Gospel of John	24
The Acts of the Apostles	70
Romans	35
I Corinthians	41
II Corinthians	17
Galatians	18
Ephesians	15
Philippians	4

Colossians	2
I Thessalonians	5
II Thessalonians	3
I Timothy	4
II Timothy	3
Titus	1
Philemon	1
Hebrews	12
James	2
I Peter	9
II Peter	1
I John	13
Jude	2
Revelation	23
	385

According to most critical Greek texts, eleven passages containing the word "spirit" should have it omitted: Matthew 14:26; Mark 6:49; Luke 2:40; Luke 9:55; Acts 18:5; Romans 8:1; I Corinthians 6:20; Ephesians 5:9; I Timothy 4:12; I Peter 1:22; I John 5:7.

According to these same critical Greek texts, three passages should have the word *pneuma*, "spirit," added: Acts 4:25; Philippians 4:23; Revelation 22:6.

How the Words *Pneuma* and *Pneuma Hagion* are Used

The following are the different forms of the word *pneuma*, "spirit," employed in the critical Greek New Testaments.

1. Used as *pneuma*, "spirit"

2. Used with the article: the *pneuma*, "the spirit"

3. Used with pronouns: my *pneuma*, "my spirit"; of, the *pneuma* of me, "the spirit of me," Matthew 12:18

4. Used with prepositions: "with," "by" or "through" the spirit

5. Used adverbially "spiritually," Acts 18:25

6. Used as *pneuma hagion*, "holy spirit," Matthew 1:18

7. Used as *hagion pneuma*, "spirit holy," I Corinthians 6:19

8. Used as the *hagion pneuma*, "the spirit holy," Matthew 28:19

9. Used as the *pneuma* the *hagion*, "the holy the spirit," Matthew 12:32

10. Used in combination with divine names for the new birth a number of different ways: *pneuma theou*, "Spirit of God," Romans 8:14; for it is God who created it — Colossians 3:10b; the new birth is His workmanship, Ephesians 2:10a; Romans 8:19; I Corinthians 3:16; II Peter 1:4

also called

pneuma christou, "Spirit of Christ" or "Christ's Spirit" because it is "Christ in you," Colossians 1:27; Romans 8:9,17

11. Used with nouns in the genitive case: sonship *pneuma*, "sonship spirit" or "spirit of sonship" — Romans 8:15 — because with "Christ in us" we are "sons of God," I John 3:2

pneuma of glory, I Peter 4:14

pneuma of holiness, Romans 1:4

pneuma of the Lord, Acts 5:9

Thus far we have given the use of the word *pneuma* in eleven major ways. Now we must still concern ourselves with the article "the" in connection with it.

The reason for its omission or its use can be determined only by a study of the entire context. In English the article "the" is frequently required in order to make good sense, yet the critical Greek texts may not have the article. In the original Estrangelo Aramaic there is no article "the" and some scholars believe that Estrangelo Aramaic was the original language and Greek a translation.

Usage of the Words *Pneuma* and *Pneuma Hagion*

The following are variations of the sense of the word *pneuma*, "spirit." The meanings are employed in New Testament usage:

1. Meaning God. God is *pneuma*, Spirit, John 4:24. God is *hagion*, Holy. I Samuel 6:20. Thus, the Holy Spirit is God.

   a. The *Giver*; God as the Giver of gifts by His divine grace and will; God to man.

2. Meaning spiritual abilities given by God.

   a. The new birth and receiving, *dechomai*, the *pneuma hagion*. This was *foretold* by Jesus in the Gospels, but was not then a reality, because Christ had not yet accomplished His mission. Jesus Christ came to make the new birth available, but it was not available until all had been fulfilled. After the death, resurrection and ascension of Jesus, and "when the day of Pentecost was fully come," the new birth and the receiving of *pneuma hagion* were available for the first time not as formerly, *upon* the believer, but now *within* every born-again believer, as "Christ in you," eternal life, born of His seed which is incorruptible (I Peter 1:23).

This gift is called *pneuma hagion*, because it is from God and God gave the greatest He is, Holy and Spirit. Thus His gift is holy spirit, which is described by the words "power," *dunamis*, inherent, latent spiritual power, "from on high," including not only the ability to operate the seven manifestations of the *pneuma* listed under 2c, but also the "speaking in tongues and interpretation of tongues," thus completing the nine manifestations of the spirit. The new birth is produced by the operation of the Holy Spirit who is God. "That which is born of the Spirit [*pneuma*, God] is spirit [*pneuma*, new birth]" (John 3:6b).

b. Ministries. A prophet is a man of God, called by God, who speaks for God, and whose *charisma* ministry is a gift of grace from God. Since Pentecost, there are five gift ministries in the Church as named in Ephesians 4:11: apostles, prophets, evangelists, pastors and teachers.

c. His *pneuma upon* certain believers (not upon *all* believers) in the Old Testament and throughout the four Gospels. This by direct appointment of the Lord. Included here we have the operation of the manifestations of prophecy, word of knowledge, word of wisdom, discerning of spirits, faith, healing and miracles. This *pneuma*, like all of God's *charismata*, is latent, potential power, until put into operation and thus manifested by the believer who has received it.

3. Meaning soul life. The person himself, that which makes man a living being; the natural life common to all mankind. It is also breath life (Luke 23:46; Acts 7:59). All men have "soul life" which is *pneuma* or spirit, called "the spirit of man," but not all men have eternal life, *pneuma*, holy spirit.

4. Meaning the individual entity or self, as myself, yourself, himself, the seat of operation of man's personal life, often referred to as "heart."

279

a. The issues that result from the operation of man's mind, such as acts of will, thoughts, desires, emotions.

5. Meaning the gift of *pneuma hagion*, holy spirit, power from on high *in manifestation* as it is given by the Giver, who is God the Holy Spirit. Note carefully the difference between No. 1 and No. 5:

Number 1 refers to the Giver of the gift.

Number 5 refers to the gift as operated by the believer, producing the manifestations of the spirit.

There are specific ways in which the Holy Spirit, the Giver, empowers His gift. This gift includes the manifestations of speaking in tongues, interpretation of tongues and prophecy, which were clearly defined in Chapter XIII. Also included in the gift are the manifestations of the word of knowledge, the word of wisdom, discerning of spirits, faith, miracles and healing. (See I Corinthians 12:8-10.) The gift from the Holy Spirit, by the *revelation* manifestations — word of knowledge, word of wisdom and discerning of spirits — gives guidance, information and direction.

a. Word of knowledge is your operation of the God-given ability to receive from God by revelation certain truths or facts concerning any situation about which it is impossible for you to know by your senses.

b. Word of wisdom is your operation of the God-given ability to receive from God, by revelation instruction as to what action to take in a specific situation after the facts or truths have been ascertained by word of knowledge. Word of wisdom is word of knowledge applied.

c. Discerning of spirits is your operation of the God-given ability to receive from God by revelation, awareness of the presence or non-presence and identity of spirits, good or evil.

The information, guidance and direction received through the revelation manifestations if applied with the *impartation* manifestations of faith (believing), miracles and healing.

d. Faith (believing) is your operation of the God-given ability to believe for the impossible to come to pass at your command as a son of God, by use of the information you have received from Him by revelation.

e. Gifts of healings is your operation of the God-given ability to impart healing wholeness by God's power in you, in the name of Jesus Christ according to the information you have received by revelation.

f. Working of miracles is your operation of the God-given ability to do miracles by His power in you, in the name of Jesus Christ, according to the revelation God has given.

Remember that the gift is the spiritual ability, God-given. There is only *one* gift, *pneuma hagion*, holy spirit. The manifestations are the result of the operation of the gift by the believer, as God the Giver activates His gift in the believer.

6. Meaning spiritual or spiritually, in the sense of reality, truly, fervently, essentially (See Romans 12:11; Acts 18:25.)

7. Meaning angels or good spirit beings (See Hebrews 1:7.)

a. Spirit body — resurrected body, a spiritual body (See I Corinthians 15:44.)

8. Meaning devil or evil spirit beings (See Matthew 10:1; Luke 4:33.)

282

a. Spirit body – spirit assuming form, in substance like ectoplasm.

9. Meaning a figure of speech.

   a. Hendiadys – two nouns in combination to mean one thing. (See Matthew 3:11: "... baptize ... with Holy Ghost [*pneuma hagion*], and *with* fire."

   b. Synecdoche – transferring one idea for an associated idea. (See Mark 16:15: "... preach the gospel to every creature" – to all people.)

   c. Metonymy – a use of one noun for another associated with or suggested by it.

   d. Idiom – an unusual usage of words or phrases, characteristic of an individual, a people or a region.

Every Use and Usage of the Words Pneuma and Pneuma Hagion in the New Testament

This section of the appendix has been added to give the student ready access to every *use* and *usage* of the word *pneuma* in the New Testament according to the critical Greek texts plus the Estrangelo Aramaic from the ancient Peshitta text, with an explanation of the usage in the light of its context. When there is a difference between the Greek and the Estrangelo Aramaic it is noted.

When the article "the" is used it is given. This procedure makes it possible for the reader to check whatever verse he is reading with the words given in the Greek and the Aramaic and come to his own conclusion. As noted earlier in the book, the words "holy," *hagion*, and "spirit," *pneuma*, are never captialized in any text, therefore the capitalization in every version is strictly private interpretation. *Pneumata* is the plural form of *pneuma*.

The following order is adhered to throughout:

First, the Scripture reference is given.

Second, the use of the word *pneuma* or *pneumata* or the words *pneuma hagion* as found in the critical Greek texts, with or without the article "the."

Third, the body of the Scripture text under consideration giving the original words for "spirit" or "holy" plus the article "the" when used.

Fourth, the explanation of the usage in the light of the context is given. The Arabic numerals refer to and agree with the numbers in Appendix II pages 275–283 under the heading of the usage of the words *pneuma* and *pneuma hagion*.

Matthew 1:18, *pneuma hagion*.
... she was found with [*en*] child of [*ek*] *pneuma hagion*.

Usage 1a
The preposition *en*, "with," governs the dative case, answering the question "with what?" – with child. The preposition *ek*, "by," governs only the genitive case and is from the interior out, answering the question "by whom?" – by God who is Holy Spirit.

Matthew 1:20, *pneuma hagion.*

... that which is conceived in her is of [by] *pneuma hagion.*

Usage 1a. Same as 1:18.

Matthew 3:11, *pneuma hagion.*

... baptize you with *pneuma hagion* and *with* fire.

Usage 2a

To be thus baptized means to be filled with the holy spirit by God the Giver, who is the Holy Spirit.

This baptism is the new birth, power from on high, a one-time occurrence for it is "Christ in you." The joined phrases "with the Holy Ghost and with fire," is hendiadys, a figure of speech using two combined terms for one intended meaning, *pneuma hagion.* "Fire" is a symbol of what the gift of the Giver will do in the "inner man," that we may be "meet for the master's use" (II Timothy 2:21), "holy and without blame" (Ephesians 1:4).

Pneuma hagion is the power given to burn up the chaff in our lives as explained in Matthew 3:12. Note: Christ "fans" to get rid of the chaff, but Satan "sifts" to get rid of the wheat (Luke 22:31). The material water of John the Baptist is to be replaced by the Spirit's baptism of Christ's presence. The dative case of "baptize" implies the element with which they were to be baptized.

This verse is foretelling. What is stated occurred for the first time on the day of Pentecost, for no one was "baptized with the spirit," the gift, before it was available, and its availability was first manifested on the day of Pentecost.

Matthew 3:16, the *pneuma*.

... he saw the *pneuma* of God descending like a dove ....

Usage 2c

Pure genitive case — genitive of origin answering the question, "whence?" The *pneuma* of God is the spirit from God as the gift proceeding from the Giver. Some of the critical Greek Texts omit the article "the" before *pneuma* and *theou*. God's *pneuma* from God the Giver was upon certain men before Pentecost because it was "with" them (John 14:17), but in Jesus' case it was upon Him as fully as it could be before Pentecost (John 3:34.)

Matthew 4:1, the *pneuma*

Then was Jesus led up of the *pneuma* ....

Usage 2c

Genitive case, preposition *hupo* — under the guidance given by the Spirit, which is given by revelation — here Jesus was "led up" by word of knowledge and wisdom. Aramaic — *roka kodsha,* or Holy Spirit.

Matthew 5:3, the *pneuma.*
Blessed are the poor in *pneuma* ....
Usage 4
Poor — humble in their own spirit, or in themselves, their own minds.
Aramaic text uses *rok*, pride, instead of *roka.*
Literal translation: "Blessed are the humble in pride," meaning they have no pride in themselves. Humble in mind which manifests itself as "pure in heart" (living) in verse 8.

Matthew 8:16, the *pneumata.*
... he cast out the *pneumata* with his word ....
Usage 8
Evil spirits which cause certain sicknesses. Aramaic text does not use *roka* (*pneumata*) but *dioa*, devils or evil spirits. Aramaic *diona* means "devil possessed," "insane, crazy, lunatic."*

Matthew 10:1, the *pneumata.*
... he gave them power (*exousia*, power to exercise) *against* unclean *pneumata* ....
Usage 8. Same as Matthew 8:16.

*According to Dr. Wierwille's discussions with Dr. George M. Lamsa, these *dioa* are wild men who do not live in society.

289

The *exousia* is the power to exercise to the end of casting out.

Matthew 10:20, the *pneuma*.

For it is not ye that speak, but the *pneuma* of your Father which speaketh in you.

Usage 2c

Your Father's *pneuma*, God, Holy Spirit.

Verse 19 tells us "it shall be given you ... what ye shall speak." The people do the speaking, but the Holy Spirit will give it to them by revelation, word of knowledge and word of wisdom. (See also Mark 13:11.) "Speaketh in you" to that which was "upon" them or "with" them, which was His gift.

Matthew 12:18, *pneuma*.

... I will put my *pneuma* upon him ....

Usage 2c

God's spirit upon him and His operation of it.

Matthew 12:28, *pneuma theou*.

... if I cast out devils by *pneuma* of God ....

Usage 2c

The spirit of God which was upon him. According to verse 18 — He cast them out by operation of the spirit which was upon Him.

Matthew 12:31, the *pneuma*.

... but the blasphemy *against* the *pneuma* shall not be forgiven ....

Usage 1

Holy Spirit, God. Unforgivable sin.

Matthew 12:32, *pneuma* the *hagion*.

... whosoever speaketh against *pneuma* the *hagion*, it shall not be forgiven him ....

Usage 1

Holy Spirit, God.

Matthew 12:43, *pneuma*.

When the unclean *pneuma* is gone out of a man ....

Usage 8. Same as Matthew 8:16.

Evil, unclean, devil spirits.

Matthew 12:45, *pneumata*.

... goeth he, and taketh with himself seven other *pneumata* more wicked than himself ....

Usage 8. Same as Matthew 8:16.

Matthew 14:26 (not *pneuma*, but *phantasma*).

... It is a *phantasma* ....

"Spirit" is not *pneuma*, but *phantasma*, an apparition or phantom.

Aramaic uses *gla*, something manifested.

291

This is the first of eleven omissions of the word *pneuma*, according to most critical Greek texts. Mark 6:49; Luke 2:40; Luke 9:55; Acts 18:5; Romans 8:1; I Corinthians 6:20; Ephesians 5:9; I Timothy 4:12; I Peter 1:22 and I John 5:7. All of these will be noted as we come to them.

Matthew 22:43, *pneuma*.

... How then doth David in *pneuma* call him Lord ....

Usage 4a. Same as Matthew 5:3.

Spirit "upon" Him whereby He spoke as the Giver, Holy Spirit, God, gave it to Him by the revelation manifestations of word of knowledge and word of wisdom. Aramaic uses it adverbially — spiritually — *brok*.

Matthew 26:41, the *pneuma*.

... the *pneuma* indeed *is* willing, but the flesh is weak.

Usage 4a. Same as Matthew 5:3

The issues emanating from the seat of man's personal life, mind, thought, will, desire, contrasting the life's desire of man with the physical man.

Matthew 27:50, the *pneuma*.

Jesus, when he had cried again with a loud voice, yielded up the *pneuma*.

Usage 3

Here *pneuma* means breath life, natural life — yielding it up He died and automatically thereby, He would give up the spirit with which God had anointed Him which then would go back to God, the Giver. Acts 10:38; Matthew 3:16,17; Luke 3:22; John 3:34.

Matthew 28:19, the *hagion pneuma*.

... baptizing them in the name of the Father, and of the Son, and of the *hagion pneuma*.

Usage 1

The Holy Spirit who is God.

There is no record in the New Testament of this clear command ever being carried out by the apostles or anyone else in the early Church. Many scholars believe that this portion was not in the original manuscripts when "holy men of God spake *as they were* moved by the Holy Spirit." The apostles always baptized in the name of Jesus Christ or of the Lord Jesus.

Acts 2:38 — "... baptized ... in the name of Jesus ...."

Acts 8:16 — "... baptized in the name of the Lord Jesus."

Acts 10:48 — "... baptized in the name of the Lord ...."

Acts 19:5 — "... baptized in the name of the Lord Jesus."

The manuscripts from which Eusebius quoted (Eusebius died in 340 A.D.) could not have used the words for he quotes Matthew 28:19 eighteen times without using them. Justin Martyr, who died in 165 A.D., never quoted these words, nor did Aphraates of Nisbis who died after 340 A.D.

Mark 1:8, *pneuma hagion*.
... he shall baptize you with *pneuma hagion*.
Usage 2a. Same as Matthew 3:11.

Mark 1:10, the *pneuma*.
... he saw the heavens opened, and the *pneuma* like a dove descending upon him.
Usage 2c. Same as Matthew 3:16.

Mark 1:12, the *pneuma*.
And immediately the *pneuma* driveth him into the wilderness.
Usage 2c. Same as Matthew 4:1.
The word "driveth" means that God let Jesus know in no uncertain terms.

Mark 1:23, *pneuma*.
... there was in their synagogue a man with an unclean *pneuma* ....
Usage 8. Same as Matthew 12:43.

Mark 1:26, the *pneuma*.
... when the unclean *pneuma* ....
Usage 8. Same as Mark 1:23.

Mark 1:27, the *pneumata*.
... with authority commandeth he even the unclean *pneumata*, and they do obey him.
Usage 8. Same as Mark 1:23.
Authority is the Greek word *exousia*, which is executed power.

Mark 2:8, *pneuma*.
... Jesus perceived in his *pneuma* ....
Usage 2c. Same as Matthew 4:1.
The Scribes were "reasoning in their hearts" which Jesus could not have known with His senses eyes, therefore it had to have been revealed to Him by word of knowledge.

Mark 3:11, the *pneumata*.
And the unclean *pneumata*, when they saw him, fell down before him ....
Usage 8. Same as Mark 1:26.
Meaning the men in whom these devil spirits dwelt.

Mark 3:29, the *pneuma* the *hagion*.
But he that shall blaspheme against the *pneuma* the *hagion* hath never forgiveness ....
Usage 1. Same as Matthew 12:32.

Mark 3:30, *pneuma*.
Because they said, He hath an unclean *pneuma*.
Usage 8

Mark 5:2, *pneuma*.
... there met him out of the tombs a man with an unclean *pneuma* ....
Usage 8

Mark 5:8, the *pneuma*.
... Come out of the man, *thou* unclean the *pneuma*.
Usage 8

Mark 5:13, the *pneumata*.
... And the unclean *pneumata* went out ....
Usage 8
The Aramaic is more specific — *those* unclean spirits went out.

Mark 6:7, the *pneumata*.

... and gave them power over the unclean *pneumata*.

Usage 8

Mark 6:49 (not *pneuma*, but *phantasma*).

... they supposed it had been a phantasma .... The word "spirit" is not *pneuma*, but *phantasma*, an apparition or phantom. Same as Matthew 14:26.

This is the second verse where the word *pneuma*, according to most critical Greek texts is omitted.

Mark 7:25:, *pneuma*.

... a *certain* woman, whose young daughter had an unclean *pneuma* ....

Usage 8

Mark 8:12, the *pneuma*.

And he sighed deeply in the *pneuma* ....

Usage 3

Mark 9:17, *pneuma*.

... I have brought unto thee my son, which hath a dumb *pneuma*.

Usage 8

The Aramaic words are *dla mmlla roka*, "without speech spirit."

Mark 9:20, the *pneuma*.
... the *pneuma* tare him ....
Usage 8

Mark 9:25, the *pneuma*; the *pneuma*.
... Jesus ... rebuked the foul [unclean] *pneuma*,
saying unto him, *Thou* dumb and deaf *pneuma* ....
Usage 8
The Aramaic gives *krshta dla mmlla roka*, "deaf
without speech spirit."

Mark 12:36, the *pneuma* the *hagion*.
... David himself said by the *pneuma* the *hagion* ....
Usage 2c

Mark 13:11, the *pneuma* the *hagion*.
... it is not ye that speak, but the *pneuma* the
hagion.
Usage 2c

Mark 14:38, the *pneuma*.
... The *pneuma* truly *is* ready, but the flesh is weak.
Usage 4a. Same as Matthew 26:41.

Luke 1:15, *pneuma hagion.*

... he shall be filled with *pneuma hagion* ....
Usage 2c

Luke 1:17, *pneuma.*

... he shall go before him in *pneuma* and power of
Elias ....
Usage 9a
Meaning, "In powerful spirit like unto Elijah,"
emphasizing the power of the spirit that Elijah
had, and which John would also manifest as the
prophet before Jesus.

Luke 1:35, *pneuma hagion.*
And the angel answered and said unto her, *pneuma
hagion* shall come upon thee ....
Usage 1a

Luke 1:41, *pneuma hagion.*
... Elisabeth was filled with *pneuma hagion* ....
Usage 2c. Same as Luke 1:15.
The spirit was upon her and she immediately
prophesied.

Luke 1:47, *pneuma.*
And my *pneuma* hath rejoiced in God my Saviour.
Usage 9b
pneuma = "spirit of me hath rejoiced ...." Usually

the Greek pronoun forms part of the verb. When the pronoun is used in addition to the verb it becomes more emphatic, but if instead of a pronoun another noun is used it becomes even more emphatic. "Magnify" is greatly praise; "rejoice" is spiritually delighted.

Luke 1:67, *pneuma hagion.*
And his [John's] father Zacharias was filled with *pneuma hagion*, and prophesied ....
Usage 2c

Luke 1:80, *pneuma.*
And the child grew, and waxed strong in *pneuma* ....
Usage 6
Dative case — "in" is not a preposition here.

Luke 2:25, *pneuma hagion.*
... *pneuma hagion* was upon him.
Usage 2c
The spirit was upon him and he prophesied as explained in Appendix II.

Luke 2:26, the *pneuma* the *hagion.*
And it was revealed unto him by the *pneuma*, the *hagion* ....
Usage 2c

300

Luke 2:27, the *pneuma.*

> And he came by the *pneuma* into the temple ....
> Usage 2c

Luke 2:40.

> And the child grew and waxed strong, filled with wisdom ....
> This is the third omission of the word *pneuma*, according to most critical Greek texts.
> Aramaic text includes "spirit," *roka.*

Luke 3:16, *pneuma hagion.*

> ... he shall baptize you with *pneuma hagion* ....
> Usage 2a. Same as Mark 1:8; Matthew 3:11

Luke 3:22, the *pneuma* the *hagion.*

> ... the *pneuma* the *hagion* descended ....
> Usage 2c
> Same as Mark 1:10; Matthew 3:16.

Luke 4:1, *pneuma hagion*; the *pneuma.*

> And Jesus being full of *pneuma hagion* returned from Jordan, and was led by the *pneuma* into the wilderness.
> Usage 2c. Same as Mark 1:12.

Luke 4:14, the *pneuma.*

> ... Jesus returned in the power of the *pneuma* ....
> Usage 2c or 9a

Jesus returned to Galilee according to the revelation which God gave him, which was spiritually powerful, as it is explained in the context of the balance of the verse and verse 15 following.

Luke 4:18, *pneuma*.
> ... *pneuma* of the Lord *is* upon me ....
>> Usage 2c
>> Aramaic text, "compelled by the spirit."

Luke 4:33, *pneuma*.
> And in the synagogue there was a man, which had a *pneuma* of an unclean devil ....
>> Usage 8. Same as Mark 1:23.
>> Aramaic text "had a sickness caused by a devil."

Luke 4:36, the *pneumata*.
> ... he commandeth the unclean *pneumata*, and they came out.
>> Usage 8

Luke 6:18, *pneumata*.
> And they that were vexed with unclean *pneumata* ....
>> Usage 8. Same as Mark 1:27.

Luke 7:21, *pneumata*.
> ... he cured many of *their* infirmities and plagues,

and of evil *pneumata* ....
Usage 8

Luke 8:2, *pneumata*.
And certain women, which had been healed of evil *pneumata* ....
Usage 8

Luke 8:29, the *pneuma*.
For he had commanded the unclean *pneuma* to come out of the man ....
Usage 8

Luke 8:55, *pneuma*.
And her *pneuma* came again ....
Usage 3

Luke 9:39, *pneuma*.
... lo, a *pneuma* taketh him ....
Usage 8

Luke 9:42, the *pneuma*.
... Jesus rebuked the unclean *pneuma* ....
Usage 8

Luke 9:55.
But he turned, and rebuked them ... [the balance of verse 55 and verse 56 is omitted to]. And they went to another village.

This is the fourth verse where the word *pneuma* according to most Greek texts is omitted. The Aramaic text includes it.*

Luke 10:20, the *pneumata*.
... rejoice not, that the *pneumata* are subject unto you ....
    Usage 8
    The Aramaic uses the word *shada*, devils.†

Luke 10:21, *pneuma*.
... Jesus rejoiced in *the pneuma* ....
    Usage 3
    Some critical Greek texts add *the hagion* and the preposition *en*, "by" — "Jesus rejoiced by the holy, the *pneuma*."
    Here Jesus rejoiced within Himself, because of the spirit from God which was upon Him, which was manifested in casting out devils and other works. "By holy spirit" is in the Aramaic text.

Luke 11:13, *pneuma hagion*.
... shall *your* heavenly Father give *pneuma hagion* to them that ask him?

*According to Dr. Wierwille's discussions with Dr. George M. Lamsa, the Aramaic says "... knowing not what temperament ye are of."

†According to Dr. Wierwille's discussions with Dr. George M. Lamsa, *shadna*, a derivative of *shada* means crazy, but not so crazy as to be violent. The *shadna* man does not make sense in his speech.

Usage 2a

In Matthew 7:11 *pneuma hagion* is replaced by "good things" indicating *pneuma hagion* both spiritually good and materially good.

Luke 11:24, *pneuma*.

When the unclean *pneuma* is gone out of a man ....
Usage 8

Luke 11:26, *pneumata*.

Then goeth he, and taketh *to him* seven other *pneumata* ....
Usage 8

Luke 12:10, the *hagion pneuma*.

... that blasphemeth against the *hagion pneuma* ....
Usage 1. Same as Matthew 12:31, 32.

In Aramaic verse 11 has the word *spirit* for the English word "answer" meaning "to defend or reply apologetically by way of the spirit."

Luke 12:12, the *hagion pneuma*.

For the *hagion pneuma* shall teach you ....
Usage 1
God the Giver – No. 1 will give to His gift – No. 2a and will then come into manifestation – No. 5. This is prophecy of Pentecost.

Luke 13:11, *pneuma.*

... there was a woman which had a *pneuma* of infirmity ....

Usage 8

An "evil spirit" afflicted this woman for eighteen years. There was apparently no physiological cause. This woman was made infirm by a devil spirit. The Aramaic text says "rheumatism."

Luke 23:46, *pneuma.*

... Father, into thy hands I commend my *pneuma* ....

Usage 3. Same as Matthew 27:50

The Aramaic text reads "my breath."

Luke 24:37, *pneuma.*

... supposed that they had seen a *pneuma.*

Usage 8a

Luke 24:39, *pneuma.*

... for a *pneuma* hath not flesh and bones, as ye see me have.

Usage 8a

John 1:32, the *pneuma.*

... I saw the *pneuma* descending from heaven ....

Usage 2c. Same as Matthew 3:16

John 1:33, the *pneuma*; *pneuma hagion*.

... Upon whom thou shalt see the *pneuma* descending, and remaining on him, the same is he which baptizeth with *pneuma hagion*.

Usage 2c

Pneuma is the spirit before Pentecost on Jesus. *Pneuma hagion* is gift to man on Pentecost and thereafter.

This verse is both forthtelling and foretelling.

John 3:5, *pneuma*.

... Except a man be born of water and of *pneuma*, he cannot enter into the kingdom of God.

Usage 9a

Meaning simply "spiritual water." To the woman at the well He taught that He was that water and would give that water as explained in John 7:37 − 39.

John 3:6, the *pneuma*; *pneuma*.

... that which is born of the *pneuma* is *pneuma*.

Usage 1 and 2a

That which is born of God is divine, or eternal, spirit.

John 3:8, *pneuma*; the *pneuma*.

The wind [*pneuma, spirit*] bloweth [breatheth] where it listeth [he willeth], and thou hearest the sound thereof [his voice thou hearest], but canst not tell [thou knowest not] whence it [he] cometh, and wither it [he] goeth: so [thus] is [it is with] every one that is born of the *pneuma* [who has been begotten by the *pneuma*].

Usage 1 and 2a

This is the only Scripture where the word *pneuma* is translated "wind." It cannot mean "wind" for John 6:18 uses the word *anemos* for "wind" and it could have been used here also. The wind has no will, but God has a will. Furthermore, the Bible teaches that the comings and goings of the wind can be followed, but this is not true of the *pneuma*.

Compare Ecclesiastes 11:5; 1:6; Job 1:19; Ezekiel 37:9. This Scripture gives us both the Giver and His gift. How God gives the gift of the new birth and how the *pneuma* in the born-again believer moves and operates by innate knowledge.

John 3:34, the *pneuma*.

... God giveth not the *pneuma* by measure *unto him*.

Usage 2c

Jesus Christ is the only one in the Bible given the spirit without measure until the day of Pentecost, when the apostles were all filled with *pneuma hagion*. Upon whom the *pneuma* was

308

not "by measure" means it was as full as was available at that time. Jesus operated seven of the nine manifestations of the spirit, all except speaking in tongues and interpretation of tongues which were manifested on Pentecost when it fully came.

John 4:23, *pneuma*.
... shall worship the Father in *pneuma* and in truth ....
Usage 9a
The *pneuma* who is truth.
Spiritual truth emphasized to magnify the truth: to worship God truly in spirit or truly with the spirit, not with material, man-made or temporal facilities.

John 4:24, *pneuma; pneuma*.
God *is pneuma* ... must worship *him* in *pneuma* and in truth.
Usage 1 and 9a
Article "a" is omitted. God is not a Spirit among many others. He is Spirit, above, over, and beyond any and all. There is none other.

John 6:63, the *pneuma; pneuma*.
It is the *pneuma* that quickeneth; the flesh profiteth nothing: the words that I speak unto you, they are *pneuma*, and *they* are life.

Usage 2a and 9c
As the body without soul is dead, so that man without God's spirit is spiritually dead. Words without being His Words are dead words, but His Words are spiritual life. His words are spiritual life-giving *pneuma* words.

John 7:39, the *pneuma; pneuma.*
... this spake he of the *pneuma*, which they that believe on him should receive: for *pneuma* was not yet *given*; because that Jesus was not yet glorified.
Usage 2a
This is spoken concerning the new birth, the receiving of the gift of holy spirit on the day of Pentecost, which could not be received at that time, for it was not yet available. No one can get a gift from God until it is available. Christ came to make the new birth available, but it was not available until Pentecost.

John 11:33, the *pneuma.*
... Jesus ... groaned in the *pneuma* [of Him] ....
Usage 4
Meaning "deeply moved in Himself."

John 13:21, the *pneuma.*
... he was troubled in the *pneuma* ....
Usage 4a
Aramaic text, "in himself."

John 14:17, the *pneuma*.
... the *pneuma* of truth ....
Usage 2a
Spoken of the Comforter who would be the gift
as specifically stated in verse 26.

John 14:26, the *pneuma* the *hagion*.
... the Comforter, *which is* the *pneuma* the
hagion ....
Usage 2a
This is the gift of the Giver who is God, being
foretold.

John 15:26, the *pneuma*.
... the *pneuma* of truth ....
Usage 2a. Same as 14:17.

John 16:13, the *pneuma*.
... when he, the *pneuma* of truth, is come, he will
guide you into all truth ....
Usage 2a. Same as 14:17.

John 19:30, the *pneuma*.
... he ... gave up the *pneuma*.
Usage 3
Aramaic text, "gave up his breath life."

John 20:22, *pneuma hagion*.

... and saith unto them, Receive [*lambanō*] ye *pneuma hagion*.

Usage 5

Manifest the evidence of — instruction for the future receiving of the gift.

Acts 1:2, *pneuma hagion*.

... after that he through *pneuma hagion* had given commandments unto the apostles whom he had chosen.

Usage 2c

"Through" is *dia*, "by" or "proceeding from" God who gave it to His spirit which was upon Jesus Christ.

Acts 1:5, *pneuma hagion*.

... but ye shall be baptized with *pneuma hagion* not many days hence.

Usage 2a

"With" is *en*, "in," not material water, but something far better, *pneuma hagion*.

Acts 1:8, the *hagion pneuma*.

... ye shall receive [*lambanō*] power [*dunamis*], after [when] that the *hagion pneuma* is come upon you: and ye shall be witnesses unto me ....

Usage 2a and 5

The opening part of this verse is the gift in

312

operation after the latter part which is the receiving of the gift.

Acts 1:16, the *pneuma* the *hagion*.

... this scripture must needs have been fulfilled, which the *pneuma*, the *hagion*, by the mouth of David spake before concerning Judas ....
Usage 2c

Acts 2:4, *pneuma hagion*; the *pneuma*.

... they were all filled with *pneuma hagion*, and began to speak with other tongues, as the *pneuma* gave them utterance.
Usage 2a and 1a

Acts 2:17, *pneuma*.

... I will pour out of my *pneuma* upon all flesh ....
Usage 2a
Cannot "pour out" God, but only His spirit can be poured out.

Acts 2:18, *pneuma*.

And on my servants and on my handmaidens I will pour out in those days of my *pneuma*; and they shall prophesy.
Usage 2a

Acts 2:33, the *pneuma* the *hagion*.

... having received of the Father the promise of the

313

pneuma the *hagion*, he hath shed forth this, which ye now see and hear.
Usage 2a

Acts 2:38, the *hagion pneuma*.
... ye shall receive the gift of the *hagion pneuma*.
Usage 1 or 2a
It could be the gift from the *pneuma hagion* who is God — No. 1 or
the gift of *pneuma hagion* — No. 2a.

Acts 4:8, *pneuma hagion*.
Then Peter, filled with *pneuma hagion* ....
Usage 2a and 5

Acts 4:25, *pneuma hagion*.
Who by *pneuma hagion*, by the mouth of thy servant David hast said ....
Usage 2c
This is the first of three passages where *pneuma* is to be added according to all other critical Greek texts than Stephens. It is in the Aramaic. Also Philippians 4:23 and Revelation 22:6. These will be noted as we come to the scriptures.

Acts 4:31, *pneuma hagion*.
... they were all filled with *pneuma hagion* ....
Usage 2a

Acts 5:3, the *pneuma* the *hagion*.

... why hath Satan filled thine heart [for] to lie to the *pneuma* the *hagion* ....

Usage 1

Acts 5:9, the *pneuma*.

... How is it that ye have agreed together to tempt the *pneuma* of the Lord?

Usage 1

Acts 5:16, *pneumata*.

... them which were vexed with unclean *pneumata* ....

Usage 8

Acts 5:32, the *pneuma* the *hagion*.

And we are his witnesses of these things; and *so is* also the *pneuma* the *hagion* ....

Usage 1

Acts 6:3, *pneuma*.

... look ye out among you seven men ... full of *pneuma* and wisdom ....

Usage 5 and 9a

Wise spiritually.

Acts 6:5, *pneuma hagion*.

... and they chose Stephen, a man full of faith and of *pneuma hagion* ....

Usage 5 and 9a
Spiritual believing.

Acts 6:10, the *pneuma*.
    ... the *pneuma* by which he spake.
    Usage 2a

Acts 7:51, the *pneuma* the *hagion*.
    ... ye do always resist the *pneuma* the *hagion* ....
    Usage 1

Acts 7:55, *pneuma hagion*.
    But he, being full of *pneuma hagion* ...
    Usage 5

Acts 7:59, *pneuma*.
    And they stoned Stephen, calling upon *God*, and
    saying, Lord Jesus, receive my *pneuma*.
    Usage 3

Acts 8:7, *pneumata*.
    For unclean *pneumata*, crying with loud voice,
    came out of many ....
    Usage 8

Acts 8:15, *pneuma hagion*.
    Who, when they were come down, prayed for
    them, that they might receive [*lambanō*] *pneuma
    hagion*.
    Usage 5

316

Acts 8:17, *pneuma hagion*.
Then laid they *their* hands on them, and they received [*lambanō*] *pneuma hagion*.
Usage 5

Acts 8:18, the *pneuma* the *hagion*.
... When Simon saw that through laying on of the apostles' hands the *pneuma* the *hagion* was given ....
Usage 5

Acts 8:19, *pneuma hagion*.
... Give me also this power, that on whomsoever I lay hands, he may receive [*lambanō*] *pneuma hagion*.
Usage 5

Acts 8:29, the *pneuma*.
Then the *pneuma* said unto Philip ....
Usage 1 via 5

Acts 8:39, *pneuma*.
... *pneuma* of the Lord caught away Philip ....
Usage 1 or 7.

Acts 9:17, *pneuma hagion*.
... and be filled with *pneuma hagion*.
Usage 5

317

Acts 9:31, the *hagion pneuma*.
Then had the churches rest throughout all
Judea ... and walking .... in the comfort of the
hagion pneuma, were multiplied.
Usage 2a and 5

Acts 10:19, the *pneuma*.
While Peter thought on the vision, the *pneuma* said
unto him ....
Usage 1 via 5

Acts 10:38, *pneuma hagion*.
How God anointed Jesus of Nazareth with *pneuma
hagion* and with power ....
Usage 2c and 9a

Acts 10:44, the *pneuma* the *hagion*.
While Peter yet spake these words, the *pneuma* the
hagion fell on all them which heard the Word.
Usage 2a

Acts 10:45, *hagion pneuma*.
... on the Gentiles also was poured out the gift of
hagion pneuma.
Usage 1 or 2a
The gift from God or the gift which is *pneuma
hagion*.

Acts 10:47, the *pneuma* the *hagion*.

318

... these ... which have received [*lambanō*] the *pneuma* the *hagion* as well as we?
Usage 5

Acts 11:12, the *pneuma*.
... the *pneuma* bade me go with them ....
Usage 1 via 5

Acts 11:15, the *pneuma* the *hagion*.
And as I began to speak, the *pneuma* the *hagion* fell on them ....
Usage 2a

Acts 11:16, *pneuma hagion*.
... ye shall be baptized with *pneuma hagion*.
Usage 2a

Acts 11:24, *pneuma hagion*.
... he was a good man, and full of *pneuma hagion* and of faith ....
Usage 2a and 9c

Acts 11:28, the *pneuma*.
... Agabus, and signified by the *pneuma* ....
Usage 5 or 6

Acts 13:2, the *pneuma* the *hagion*.
... the *pneuma* the *hagion* said, Separate me

Barnabas and Saul for the work whereunto I have called them.
    Usage 1 via 5

Acts 13:4, the *pneuma* the *hagion*.
    So they, being sent for by the *pneuma* the *hagion*, departed ....
    Usage 1 via 5

Acts 13:9, *pneuma hagion*.
    Then Saul ... filled with *pneuma hagion*, set his eyes on him ....
    Usage 5

Acts 13:52, *pneuma hagion*.
    ... the disciples were filled with joy, and with *pneuma hagion*.
    Usage 5

Acts 15:8, *pneuma hagion*.
    ... God, which knoweth the hearts, bare them witness, giving them the *pneuma* the *hagion* ....
    Usage 2a

Acts 15:28, the *pneuma* the *hagion*.
    ... it seemed good to the *pneuma*, the *hagion*, and to us ....
    Usage 1 via 5

Acts 16:6, the *hagion pneuma*.

... they ... were forbidden of the *hagion pneuma* to preach the word in Asia.

Usage 1 via 5

Acts 16:7, the *pneuma*.

... the *pneuma* suffered them not.

Usage 1 via 5

Acts 16:16, *pneuma*.

... a *pneuma* of divination [Python] ....

Usage 8

Acts 16:18, the *pneuma*.

... Paul ... said to the *pneuma* ....

Usage 8

Acts 17:16, the *pneuma*.

... while Paul waited for them at Athens, the *pneuma* was stirred in him ....

Usage 4a or 5

Acts 18:5.

Paul was [the Greek says — was engrossed with The Word] ....

Omitted by all other critical Greek texts and the Aramaic. Fifth Scripture where the word *pneuma* is omitted.

Acts 18:25, the *pneuma*.

... and being fervent in the *pneuma* ....
Usage 6

Acts 19:2, *pneuma hagion; pneuma hagion*.

... Have ye received [*lambanō*] *pneuma hagion* since ye believed? And they said ... We have not ... heard whether there be any *pneuma hagion*.
Usage 5

Acts 19:6, the *pneuma* the *hagion*.

And when Paul had laid *his* hands upon them, the *pneuma* the *hagion* came on them; and they spake with tongues, and prophesied.
Usage 5
Came into manifestation.

Acts 19:12, *pneumata*.

... the evil *pneumata* went out of them.
Usage 8
Aramaic has *shada* meaning "devils" or "evil spirits."*

Acts 19:13, *pneumata*.

... took upon them to call over them which had evil *pneumata* ....
Usage 8

*According to Dr. Wierwille's discussions with Dr. George M. Lamsa, *shada* usually carries the meaning of crazy.

Acts 19:15, *pneuma*.

... the evil *pneuma* answered and said ....
    Usage 8. Same as Acts 19:12.

Acts 19:16, *pneuma*.

... the man in whom the evil *pneuma* was leaped on
them ....
    Usage 8

Acts 19:21, the *pneuma*.

... Paul purposed in his *pneuma* ....
    Usage 4
    In the Aramaic the word *pneuma* does not
    appear but the word "mind," *rāina.*

Acts 20:22, the *pneuma*.

And now, behold, I go bound in the [as to]
pneuma ....
    Usage 4a or 5
    Word of knowledge was, "Do not go." Paul him-
    self wanted to go — thus he was not free; he was
    "bound in the spirit."

Acts 20:23, the *pneuma* the *hagion*.

... the *pneuma* the *hagion* witnesseth in every city,
saying that bonds and afflictions abide me.
    Usage 5

Acts 20:28, the *pneuma* the *hagion*.

... the flock, over the which the *pneuma* the *hagion* hath made you overseers ....

Usage 1

Acts 21:4, the *pneuma*.

... disciples ... who said to Paul through the *pneuma* ....

Usage 5

Acts 21:11, the *pneuma*, the *hagion*.

... Thus saith the *pneuma* the *hagion* ....

Usage 1 via 5

Acts 23:8, *pneuma*.

... the Sadducees say that there is ... neither angel, nor *pneuma*....

Usage 7 and 8

Acts 23:9, *pneuma*.

... if a *pneuma* or an angel hath spoken to him, let us not fight against God.

Usage 1

Acts 28:25, the *pneuma* the *hagion*.

... Well spake the *pneuma* the *hagion* by Essias the prophet ....

Usage 1 via 2c

Romans 1:4, *pneuma hagiosunēs*.

324

... declared *to be* the Son of God with power, according to *pneuma hagiosunēs* ....
Usage 1

Romans 1:9, *pneuma.*
... God is my witness, whom I serve with my *pneuma* ....
Usage 4 or 6

Romans 2:29, *pneuma.*
... and circumcision *is that* of the heart, in *pneuma, and* not in the letter ....
Usage 2a or 9c

Romans 5:5, *pneuma hagion.*
... the love of God is shed abroad in our hearts by *pneuma hagion* which is given unto us.
Usage 2a

Romans 7:6 *pneuma.*
... that we should serve in newness of *pneuma* ....
Usage 2a or 6

Romans 8:1
There is therefore now no condemnation to them which are in Christ Jesus [rest of verse omitted].
This is the sixth omission of the word *pneuma.* It is also omitted in the Aramaic text.

Romans 8:2, the *pneuma*.

For the law of the *pneuma* of life in Christ Jesus hath made me free from the law of sin and death.
Usage 2a via 9c

Romans 8:4, *pneuma*.

... of the law might be fulfilled in us, who walk not after the flesh, but after [according to] *pneuma*.
Usage 5

Romans 8:5 *pneuma*; the *pneuma*.

... but they that are after [according to] *pneuma* [do mind] the things of the *pneuma*.
Usage 5 and 1

Romans 8:6, the *pneuma*.

For to be carnally minded *is* [the mind of the flesh] death; but to be the *pneuma* minded *is* life and peace.
Usage 6
This is the spiritually renewed mind.

Romans 8:9, *pneuma; pneuma theou; pneuma christou*.

... ye are not in the flesh, but in *pneuma*, if so be that *pneuma theou* dwell in you. Now [but] if any man have not *pneuma christou*, he is none of his.
Usage 2a

Romans 8:10, the *pneuma*.

... but the *pneuma is* life because [on account] of righteousness.

Usage 2a

Romans 8:11, the *pneuma, pneuma.*

But [and] if the *pneuma* of him that raised up Jesus from [among] the dead dwell in you, he that raised up Christ from [among] the dead shall also quicken your mortal bodies [also] by [on account of] his *pneuma* that dwelleth in you.

Usage 2a and 5

Romans 8:13, *pneuma.*

... but if ye through [by] *pneuma* do mortify [ye are putting to death by reckoning] the deeds of the body, ye shall live.

Usage 4a

Spiritually renewed mind.

Romans 8:14, *pneuma theou.*

For as many as are led by *pneuma theou*, they are the sons of God.

Usage 5

Romans 8:15, *pneuma; pneuma.*

For ye have not received a bondage *pneuma*, again to [unto] fear: but ye have received a sonship *pneuma* ....

327

Usage 8 first; 2a second

According to all critical Greek texts it is a sonship spirit instead of a spirit of adoption.

Romans 8:16, the *pneuma*; the *pneuma*.

The *pneuma* itself beareth witness with our the *pneuma*, that we are the children of God.

Usage 1 via 5

Romans 8:23, the *pneuma*.

... but ourselves also, which have the first fruits of the *pneuma* ....

Usage 2a

Which have Christ who is the "first fruits."

Romans 8:26, the *pneuma*; the *pneuma*.

Likewise the *pneuma* also helpeth our infirmities: for we know not what we should pray for as we ought: but the *pneuma* itself maketh intercession for us ....

Usage 1 and 5

Romans 8:27, the *pneuma*.

... he that searcheth the hearts knoweth what *is* the mind of the *pneuma* ....

Usage 4a or 5

Romans 9:1, *pneuma hagion*.

... my conscience also bearing me witness in [with]

pneuma hagion ....
Usage 5

Romans 11:8, *pneuma*.
... God hath given [permitted] them the *pneuma* of slumber [spiritual blindness] ....
Usage 8

Romans 12:11, the *pneuma*.
... fervent in the *pneuma* ....
Usage 6
Spiritually fervent.

Romans 14:17, *pneuma hagion*.
... righteousness, and peace, and joy in [through] *pneuma hagion*.
Usage 2a
Joy in the new birth.

Romans 15:13, *pneuma hagion*.
... that ye may abound in hope, through the power of *pneuma hagion*.
Usage 2a or 5

Romans 15:16, *pneuma hagion*.
... being sanctified by *pneuma hagion*.
Usage 1

Romans 15:19, *pneuma hagion.*
Through mighty signs and wonders, by the power of *pneuma hagion* ....
Usage 5
The Aramaic text has "spirit of God."

Romans 15:30, the *pneuma.*
Now I beseech you, brethren, for [by] the [our] Lord Jesus Christ's sake, and for [by] the love of the *pneuma* ....
Usage 6
Spiritual love for Paul.

I Corinthians 2:4, *pneuma.*
... my speech and my preaching *was* not with enticing words of man's [human] wisdom, but in demonstration of *pneuma* and of power.
Usage 5 and 9a

I Corinthians 2:10, the *pneuma*; the *pneuma.*
But God hath revealed them unto us by the *pneuma*: for the *pneuma* searcheth all things, yea, the deep things of God.
Usage 5

I Corinthians 2:11, the *pneuma*; the *pneuma.*
For what man knoweth the [deep] things of a man, save the *pneuma* of man which is in him? even to the [deep] things of God knoweth no man,

but the *pneuma* of God.
    Usage 4 and 1

I Corinthians 2:12, the *pneuma*; the *pneuma*.
    Now we have received, not the *pneuma* of the world, but the *pneuma* which is of God ....
    Usage 8 and 2a

I Corinthians 2:13, the *pneuma*.
    ... not in [with] the words which man's wisdom teacheth, but which [with those words] *pneuma hagion* teacheth ....
    Usage 5
    The word *hagion* is omitted in all critical Greek texts except Stephens. Not in the Aramaic.

I Corinthians 2:14, the *pneuma*.
    ... the natural man receiveth not the things of the *pneuma* of God ....
    Usage 1

I Corinthians 3:16, the *pneuma*.
    Know ye not that ye are the temple of God, and *that* the *pneuma* of God dwelleth in you?
    Usage 2a

I Corinthians 4:21, *pneuma*.
    ... shall I come ... *in pneuma* of meekness?
    Usage 4a

I Corinthians 5:3, *pneuma*.

... I verily, as absent in body, but present in *pneuma* ....

Usage 4a or 5

I Corinthians 5:4, *pneuma*.

when ye are gathered together, and my *pneuma* ....

Usage 3

I Corinthians 5:5, the *pneuma*.

... that the *pneuma* may be saved in the day of the Lord Jesus.

Usage 2a

I Corinthians 6:11, the *pneuma*.

... in the name of the Lord Jesus, and by the *pneuma* of our God.

Usage 1

I Corinthians 6:17, *pneuma*.

... he that is joined unto the Lord is one *pneuma*.

Usage 2a

I Corinthians 6:19, *hagion pneuma*.

... know ye not that your body is the temple of the *hagion pneuma which is* in you ....

Usage 2a

I Corinthians 6:20.

... therefore glorify in your body [rest of verse omitted].

This is the seventh omission of the word *pneuma* by all the other critical Greek texts. It is in the Aramaic text.

I Corinthians 7:34, *pneuma*.

... that she may be holy both in body and in *pneuma* ....

Usage 6

I Corinthians 7:40, *pneuma theou*.

... I think also that I have *pneuma theou.*

Usage 2a and 5

I Corinthians 12:3, *pneuma theou; pneuma hagion*.

... no man speaking by *pneuma theou* calleth Jesus accursed: ... no man can say that Jesus is the Lord, but by *pneuma hagion.*

Usage 2a and 5

I Corinthians 12:4, the *pneuma*.

... there are diversities of gifts, but the same *pneuma*.

Usage 1

I Corinthians 12:7, the *pneuma*.

But the manifestation of the *pneuma* is given to

every man ....
Usage 5

I Corinthians 12:8, the *pneuma*; the *pneuma*.
... to one is given by the *pneuma* the word of
wisdom; to another the word of knowledge, by the
same *pneuma*.
Usage 1 via 5

I Corinthians 12:9, *pneuma*; *pneuma*.
To another faith, by the same *pneuma*; to another
the gifts of healing, by the same *pneuma*.
Usage 1 via 5

I Corinthians 12:10, *pneumata*.
... to another discerning of *pneumata* ....
Usage 8
In the Aramaic text "spirit" is singular.

I Corinthians 12:11, *pneuma*.
... all these worketh that one and the selfsame
pneuma ....
Usage 1

I Corinthians 12:13, *pneuma*; *pneuma*.
For by [with] one *pneuma* are we all baptized into
one body, ... and have been all made to drink into
one *pneuma*.
Usage 1 and 2a

I Corinthians 14:2, *pneuma*.
... howbeit in *pneuma* he speaketh mysteries.
Usage 5

I Corinthians 14:12, *pneumata*.
... forasmuch as ye are zealous of *pneumata* ....
Usage 6
In the Aramaic text "spirit" is singular.

I Corinthians 14:14, *pneuma*.
... if I pray in an *unknown* tongue, my *pneuma* prayeth ....
Usage 5

I Corinthians 14:15, the *pneuma*; the *pneuma*.
... I will pray with the *pneuma* ... I will sing with the *pneuma* ....
Usage 5

I Corinthians 14:16, the *pneuma*.
Else when thou shalt bless with the *pneuma* ....
Usage 5

I Corinthians 14:32, *pneumata*.
And the *pneumata* of the prophets are subject to the prophets.
Usage 2a and 5
In the Aramaic text "spirit" is singular.

I Corinthians 15:45, *pneuma.*

... The first man Adam was made a living soul; the last Adam *was made* a quickening *pneuma.*

Usage 7a

I Corinthians 16:18, *pneuma.*

For they have refreshed my *pneuma* and yours ....

Usage 4

II Corinthians 1:22, the *pneuma.*

Who hath also sealed us, and given the earnest of the *pneuma* in our hearts.

Usage 2a or 5

II Corinthians 2:13, *pneuma.*

I had no rest in my *pneuma* ....

Usage 4

II Corinthians 3:3, *pneuma.*

... written not with ink, but with *pneuma* of the living God ....

Usage 1

II Corinthians 3:6, *pneuma;* the *pneuma.*

... not of the letter, but of *pneuma:* for the letter killeth, but the *pneuma* giveth life.

Usage 5 and 1

336

II Corinthians 3:8, the *pneuma*.

How shall not the ministration of the *pneuma* be rather glorious?

Usage 5

II Corinthians 3:17, the *pneuma*; the *pneuma*.

Now the Lord is that *pneuma*: and where the *pneuma* [that is to say] of the Lord *is*, there *is* liberty.

Usage 1 and 5

II Corinthians 3:18, *pneuma*.

... from glory to glory [one glory reflecting another glory], *even* as by *pneuma* of the Lord [coming from the Lord who is *pneuma*].

Usage 1

II Corinthians 4:13, *pneuma*.

We having the same *pneuma* of [which is] faith ....

Usage 2a

II Corinthians 5:5, the *pneuma*.

... God, who also hath given unto us the earnest of [which is] the *pneuma*.

Usage 2a and 5

II Corinthians 6:4 − 6, *pneuma hagion*.

In all *things* approving ourselves as the ministers ... by *pneuma hagion* ....

Usage 5

II Corinthians 7:1, *pneuma*.
... let us cleanse ourselves from all filthiness of the flesh and *pneuma* ....
Usage 9b

II Corinthians 7:13, *pneuma*.
... because his *pneuma* was refreshed by you all.
Usage 4

II Corinthians 11:4, *pneuma*.
... or *if* ye receive [are receiving a different] another *pneuma* ....
Usage 8

II Corinthians 12:18, *pneuma*.
... walked we not in the same *pneuma* ....
Usage 6 and 4a

II Corinthians 13:14, the *hagion pneuma*.
... the communion of the *hagion pneuma* ....
Usage 1

Galatians 3:2, the *pneuma*.
... Received ye the *pneuma* by the works of the law ....
Usage 2a

Galatians 3:3, *pneuma*.
Are ye so foolish? having begun in *pneuma*, are ye

338

now made perfect by the flesh?
Usage 2a

Galatians 3:5, the *pneuma*.
... that ministereth to you the *pneuma*, and
worketh miracles ... *doeth he it* by the works of
the law, or by the hearing of faith?
Usage 2a

Galatians 3:14, the *pneuma*.
... that we might receive the promise of the
pneuma ....
Usage 2a

Galatians 4:6, the *pneuma*.
... God hath sent forth the *pneuma* of his Son into
your hearts ....
Usage 2a

Galatians 4:29, *pneuma*.
... he that was born after [according to] the flesh
persecuted him *that was born* after [according to]
pneuma ....
Usage 1
The meaning here is that Ishmael was born
through Abraham's trying to work out the
promise, but Isaac was born because of what
God did for Sarah, therefore, usage 1.

Galatians 5:5, *pneuma*.

For we through [by] *pneuma* wait for the hope of righteousness by faith.

Usage 1

By the power of God we are awaiting Christ who is our hope of righteousness. This we are doing by the believing of His Word.

Galatians 5:16, *pneuma*.

This I say then, Walk in [by] *pneuma* ....

Usage 5

Galatians 5:17, the *pneuma*; the *pneuma*.

For the flesh lusteth against the *pneuma*, and the *pneuma* against the flesh ....

Usage 5

Galatians 5:18, *pneuma*.

But if ye be led of [by] *pneuma*, ye are not under the law.

Usage 5

Galatians 5:22, the *pneuma*.

... the fruit of the *pneuma* ....

Usage 5

Galatians 5:25, *pneuma; pneuma*.

If we live in [by] *pneuma,* let us also walk in [by] *pneuma.*

Usage 2a and 5

Galatians 6:1, *pneuma*.

   ... restore such an one in the *pneuma* of meekness ....

   Usage 6 and 9c

Galatians 6:8, the *pneuma*; the *pneuma*.

   ... he that soweth to the *pneuma* shall of the *pneuma* reap life everlasting.

   Usage 5 and 1

Galatians 6:18, the *pneuma*.

   ... the grace of our Lord Jesus Christ *be* with your *pneuma* ....

   Usage 3 or 4

Ephesians 1:13, the *pneuma* the *hagion*.

   ... we were sealed with that the *pneuma* the *hagion* of promise.

   Usage 2a via 1 plus 5

   Literally sealed by the *pneuma* who is God.

Ephesians 1:17, *pneuma*.

   ... may give unto you *pneuma* [that is to say] of wisdom and revelation in the knowledge of him.

   Usage 6 or 9c

   Spiritual wisdom and revelation knowledge.

Ephesians 2:2, the *pneuma*.

   ... the *pneuma* that now worketh in the children of disobedience ....

   Usage 8

Ephesians 2:18, *pneuma.*

... through him we both have access by one *pneuma* unto the Father.

Usage 2a

Both Jews and Gentiles have access unto the Father by the new birth.

Ephesians 2:22, *pneuma.*

... for an habitation of God through [by way of] *pneuma.*

Usage 1

Ephesians 3:5, *pneuma.*

... unto his holy apostles and prophets by *pneuma* ....

Usage 5

Ephesians 3:16, the *pneuma.*

... to be strengthened with might by his the *pneuma* [of Him] in the inner man.

Usage 5

Ephesians 4:3, the *pneuma.*

Endeavouring to keep the unity of the *pneuma* ....

Usage 6

Spiritually united.

Ephesians 4:4, *pneuma.*

There is one body, and one *pneuma* ....

Usage 1 and 2a

The one body is the Church and all in the Church (born-again believers) have one *pneuma*.

Ephesians 4:23, the *pneuma*.

... be renewed in the *pneuma* [that is to say] of your mind ....

Usage 4a

Ephesians 4:30, the *pneuma* the *hagion*.

And grieve not the *pneuma*, the *hagion*, of God whereby [by whom] ye are sealed ....

Usage 1

Do not offend or grieve God who is Holy Spirit by breaking the unity of the Spirit as indicated in verses 31 and 32.

Ephesians 5:9.

(For the fruit of the light is in all goodness and righteousness and truth.)

This is the eighth omission by all critical Greek texts except Stephens. Also omitted in Aramaic.

Ephesians 5:18, *pneuma*.

... be not drunk with wine, wherein is excess; but be filled with [by] *pneuma*;

Usage 2a and 5

343

Ephesians 6:17, the *pneuma*.
... the sword of the *pneuma* ....
   Usage 1
   The sword of God is The Word, either written or
   incarnate.

Ephesians 6:18, *pneuma*.
   Praying always with all prayer and supplication in
   [by way of] *pneuma* ....
   Usage 5

Philippians 1:19, the *pneuma*.
   For I know that this shall turn to my salvation
   [deliverance from bonds] through your prayer,
   and the supply of the *pneuma* of [by] Jesus Christ.
   Usage 2a

Philippians 1:27, *pneuma*.
   ... that ye stand fast in one *pneuma* ....
   Usage 6
   Stand fast as one, spiritually.

Philippians 2:1, *pneuma*.
   ... if [there be] any fellowship of *pneuma* ....
   Usage 6
   Any spiritual fellowship.

Philippians 3:3, *pneuma theou*.
   For we are the circumcision, which worship God in

[by way of] *pneuma theou* ....
    Usage 5

Philippians 4:23, the *pneuma*.
    The grace of our Lord Jesus Christ *be* with your
    the *pneuma* ....
    Usage 3
    This is the second addition of *pneuma* according
    to all critical Greek texts except the Stephens
    and Griesbach. The Aramaic omits it and reads
    "with you all."

Colossians 1:8, *pneuma*.
    Who also declared unto us your love in *pneuma*.
    Usage 6
    Your spiritual love for us.

Colossians 2:5, the *pneuma*.
    For though I be absent in the flesh, yet am I with
    you in the *pneuma*....
    Usage 4a or 5

I Thessalonians 1:5, *pneuma hagion*.
    For our gospel came not unto you in word only,
    but also in power, and in *pneuma hagion* ....
    Usage 5 and 9a

I Thessalonians 1:6, *pneuma hagion*.
    ... having received the word in much affliction,

with joy of *pneuma hagion*.
> Usage 2a

I Thessalonians 4:8, the *pneuma* the *hagion*.
> ... but God, who hath also given unto us his the *pneuma* the *hagion*.
> Usage 2a

I Thessalonians 5:19, the *pneuma*.
> Quench not the *pneuma*.
> Usage 5

I Thessalonians 5:23, the *pneuma*.
> ... and *I pray God* your whole the *pneuma* and soul and body be preserved blameless ....
> Usage 2a

II Thessalonians 2:2, *pneuma*.
> ... not soon shaken in mind, or be troubled, neither by *pneuma*, nor by word, nor by letter, as from us ....
> Usage 8
> Devil spirits operating through men's lips saying that the day of Christ is at hand.

II Thessalonians 2:8, the *pneuma*.
> ... whom the Lord shall consume [destroy] with the *pneuma* of his mouth ....

346

Usage 9d
An Aramaic idiom for "breath of our Lord Jesus."

II Thessalonians 2:13, *pneuma*.
... salvation through [by way of] sanctification of *pneuma* ....
Usage 2a

I Timothy 3:16, *pneuma*.
... God was manifest in the flesh, justified in *pneuma* ....
Usage 6
Spiritually justified

I Timothy 4:1, the *pneuma; pneumata*.
Now the *pneuma* speaketh expressly, that in the latter times some shall depart from the faith, giving heed to seducing [deceiving] *pneumata*, and doctrines [teachings] of devils.
Usage 1 and 8

I Timothy 4:12.
... in word, in conversation, in charity, in faith, in purity.

The ninth omission of the word *pneuma* by all critical Greek texts except Stephens. Also omitted in Aramaic.

II Timothy 1:7, *pneuma.*
For God hath not given us *pneuma* of fear.
Usage 8
A spirit of cowardice according to all critical Greek texts.

II Timothy 1:14, *pneuma hagion.*
That good thing [good deposit] ... keep by *pneuma hagion* which dwelleth in us.
Usage 5

II Timothy 4:22, the *pneuma.*
The Lord ... *be* with thy the *pneuma* ....
Usage 3 or 6
The Lord be with you all.
or
The Lord be with all of you spiritually.

Titus 3:5, *pneuma hagion.*
... and renewing [even the new creation] of *pneuma hagion* ....
Usage 2a

Philemon, verse 25, the *pneuma.*
The grace of our Lord Jesus Christ *be* with your the *pneuma.*
Usage 6
Be with you spiritually.

348

Hebrews 1:7, *pneumata*.

... Who maketh his angels *pneumata* ....

Usage 7

Hebrews 1:14, *pneumata*.

Are they not all ministering *pneumata* ....

Usage 7

These minister to the "believers to be" before salvation. After salvation we have *pneuma hagion* in us to do the ministering.

Hebrews 2:4, *pneuma hagion*.

... both with signs and wonders, and with divers miracles, and gifts of *pneuma hagion* ....

Usage 2b

Ministries here — Ephesians 4:11.

Hebrews 3:7, the *pneuma* the *hagion*.

Wherefore (as the *pneuma* the *hagion* saith, To day if ye will hear his voice.

Usage 1

By the prophets of old — spoken by Holy Ghost.

Hebrews 4:12, *pneuma*.

... piercing even to the dividing asunder of soul and *pneuma* ....

Usage 2a

Dividing natural life and new birth or spiritual life.

Hebrews 6:4, *pneuma hagion.*

... and have tasted of the heavenly gift, and were made partakers of *pneuma hagion.*

Usage 2a

Hebrews 9:8, the *pneuma*, the *hagion.*

The *pneuma* the *hagion* this signifying ....

Usage 1

Hebrews 9:14, *pneuma.*

... who through eternal *pneuma* offered himself without spot to God ....

Usage 1

Hebrews 10:15, the *pneuma* the *hagion.*

Whereof the *pneuma* the *hagion* also is a witness to us ....

Usage 1

Hebrews 10:29, the *pneuma.*

... and hath done despite unto the *pneuma* of grace?

Usage 1

Hebrews 12:9, the *pneumata.*

... shall we not much rather be in subjection unto the Father of the *pneumata*, and live?

Usage 1

Hebrews 12:23, *pneumata*.

... and to God the Judge of all, and to *pneumata* of just men made perfect.

Usage 2a

James 2:26, *pneuma*.

For as the body without *pneuma* is dead, so faith without works is dead also.

Usage 3

James 4:5, the *pneuma*.

Do ye think that the scripture saith in vain, The *pneuma* that dwelleth in us lusteth to envy?

Usage 3

I Peter 1:2, *pneuma*.

... through sanctification of [by] *pneuma* ....

Usage 2a

I Peter 1:11, the *pneuma*.

Searching what, or what manner of time the *pneuma* of Christ which was in them did signify ....

Usage 2c

I Peter 1:12, *pneuma hagion*.

... reported unto you by them that have preached the gospel unto you with *pneuma hagion* sent down from heaven ....

Usage 5

351

I Peter 1:22.

... obeying the truth unto unfeigned love of the brethren ....

Tenth omission of the word *pneuma* in all the critical Greek texts, except Stephens and Griesbach. Omitted in Aramaic also.

I Peter 3:4, *pneuma*.

... *even the ornament* of a meek and quiet *pneuma* ....

Usage 6 and 9a

Spiritually meek and tranquil.

I Peter 3:18, *pneuma*.

... being put to death in the flesh, but quickened [made alive] by *pneuma*.

Usage 7a

I Peter 3:19, *pneumata*.

By which [resurrection body] also he went and preached [proclaimed] unto *pneumata* in prison.

Usage 8

I Peter 4:6, *pneuma*.

... that they might be judged according to [the will of] men in the flesh, but live [again] according to the will of God in *pneuma*.

Usage 7a

I Peter 4:14, the *pneuma*.

... happy *are ye*; for the *pneuma* of glory and of God resteth upon you ....

Usage 1 and 9a

II Peter 1:21, *pneuma hagion*.

... but holy men of God spake *as they were* moved by *pneuma hagion*.

Usage 2c and 5

I John 3:24, the *pneuma*.

... And hereby we know that he abideth in us, by the *pneuma* which he hath given us.

Usage 2a and 5

I John 4:1, *pneuma*; *pneumata*.

Beloved, believe not every *pneuma*, but try the *pneumata* whether they are of God ....

Usage 2a and 8

I John 4:2, the *pneuma*; *pneuma*.

Hereby know ye the *pneuma* of God: Every *pneuma* that confesseth that Jesus Christ is come in the flesh is of God.

Usage 1 and 3

I John 4:3, *pneuma*.

And every *pneuma* that confesseth not that Jesus Christ is come in the flesh is not of God ....

Usage 3

I John 4:6, the *pneuma*, the *pneuma*.

... Hereby know we the *pneuma* of truth, and the *pneuma* of error.

Usage 1 and 8

I John 4:13, *pneuma*.

... because he hath given us of his *pneuma*.

Usage 2a and 5

I John 5:6, the *pneuma*; the *pneuma*.

... And it is the *pneuma* that beareth witness, because the *pneuma* is truth.

Usage 1

I John 5:7.

For there are three that bear record [the balance of verse 7 is omitted].

This is the eleventh omission of *pneuma hagion* in all critical Greek texts, except Stephens. The entire verse is omitted in Aramaic.

I John 5:8, the *pneuma*.

The *pneuma*, and the water, and the blood ....

Usage 2a and 5

All the first part of verse 8 is omitted in all critical Greek texts except Stephens. The Aramaic omits only the words "in earth" in this verse.

Jude, verse 19, *pneuma.*
These be they who separate themselves, sensual, [natural men] having not *pneuma.*
Usage 2a

Jude, verse 20, *pneuma hagion.*
... building up yourselves on your most holy faith, praying in [with] *pneuma hagion.*
Usage 5

Revelation 1:4, the *pneumata.*
... and from the seven *pneumata* which are before his throne.
Usage 7

Revelation 1:10, *pneuma.*
I was in *pneuma* on the Lord's Day ....
Usage 5

Revelation 2:7, 11, 17, 29, the *pneuma.*
... let him hear what the *pneuma* saith unto the churches ....
Usage 5
All four verses are the same.

Revelation 3:1, the *pneumata.*
... the seven *pneumata* of God ....
Usage 1 or 7

Revelation 3:6, 13, 22, the *pneuma*.
... let him hear what the *pneuma* saith unto the churches.
Usage 1

Revelation 4:2, *pneuma*.
And immediately I was in *pneuma* ....
Usage 5

Revelation 4:5, the *pneumata*.
... the seven *pneumata* of God.
Usage 7

Revelation 5:6, *pneumata*.
... which are the seven *pneumata* of God.
Usage 1 or 7

Revelation 11:11, *pneuma*.
And after three days and an half *pneuma* of life from God entered into them ....
Usage 1

Revelation 13:15, *pneuma*.
... he had power to give *pneuma* unto the image of the beast ....
Usage 8

Revelation 14:13, the *pneuma*.
... Yea, saith the *pneuma* ....
Usage 1

356

Revelation 16:13, *pneumata*.
  And I saw three unclean *pneumata* ....
    Usage 8

Revelation 16:14, *pneumata*.
  For they are the *pneumata* of devils ....
    Usage 8

Revelation 17:3, *pneuma*.
  So he carried me away in *pneuma* ....
    Usage 5

Revelation 18:2, *pneuma*.
  ... and the hold of every foul [unclean] *pneuma* ....
    Usage 8

Revelation 19:10, the *pneuma*.
  ... for the testimony of Jesus is the *pneuma* of prophecy.
    Usage 2c

Revelation 21:10, *pneuma*.
  And he carried me away in *pneuma* ....
    Usage 5

Revelation 22:6, the *pneumata*.
  ... and the Lord God of the *pneumata* of the prophets, sent his angel ....
    Usage 5

This is the third addition of *pneuma* according to all the critical Greek texts except Stephens. It is in the Aramaic. "Holy" is omitted.

Revelation 22:17, the *pneuma*.
And the *pneuma* and the bride say, Come ....
Usage 1

About the Author

Victor Paul Wierwille has spent many years searching, and seeking enlightenment on God's Word from men of God scattered across the continent. His academic career after high school continued at the Mission House (Lakeland) College and Seminary, Sheboygan, Wisconsin, where he received his Bachelor of Arts and Bachelor of Divinity degrees. Dr. Wierwille studied at the University of Chicago and at Princeton Theological Seminary where he was awarded the Master of Theology degree in Practical Theology. Later he completed his work for the Doctor of Theology degree.

For sixteen years Dr. Wierwille served as a pastor in northwestern Ohio. During these years he searched the Word of God for keys to powerful victorious living. Dr. Wierwille visited E. Stanley Jones and studied his Ashram program. Such men as Glenn Clark, Rufus Mosley, Starr Daily, Albert Cliffe, Bishop K.C. Pillai and others were guests of Dr. Wierwille's local congregation. Karl Barth of Switzerland was a

359

friend and consultant, as is George M. Lamsa, the
Aramaic scholar, as well as other European and Far
Eastern scholars. With these men Dr. Wierwille
quested for Biblical enlightenment. In 1953 he began
teaching classes on Power for Abundant Living. These
concentrated sessions are specifically directed to
unfold the Word of God as the Will of God and to
answer crucial questions regarding the holy spirit and
its present availability and efficacy in believers' lives.
Leading men and women from all over the world into
receiving the more abundant life quickly consumed
Dr. Wierwille's full time, so it became necessary for
him to resign his local pastorate. Since that time Dr.
Wierwille has devoted his entire energy to The Way
Biblical Research Center in New Knoxville, Ohio.
There, as elsewhere in the United States and foreign
countries, he continues to study, write and teach the
greatness of God's Word.

.